BLACK KNIGHT

from pushin dope to pushin hope

BOBBY LLOYD

With Steve Gallagher

OlivePress
צהר זית

Messianic & Christian Publisher

DEDICATION

*This book is affectionately dedicated
to our eldest son Gregory
whose life and memory
are forever engraved in our hearts and
woven in the pages of this book.*

ACKNOWLEDGMENTS

First and foremost I would like to give all the glory and the honor for this book to my Savior and Lord who knew me before the foundations of the world and saw fit to save my life and raise me up to be a minister after His own heart. I thank Him daily for all He has done in my life and the life of my family and am forever grateful for His love, mercy, and grace.

I am so grateful for my parents who did the best they could to instill in me their core values of responsibility, hard work and that I could be all that I wanted to be. I am forever thankful for Mr. and Mrs. Jack who loved and accepted me and never judged me by the color of my skin or what I did. Both of them saw something in me that I did not see in my self and believed one day I would make a difference in this world.

My wife, Dianne who has stuck by me through thick and thin at home, in ministry, in sickness and disease, and in helping me raise my children and grandchildren. This book would never have been completed with out her attention to detail and perseverance.

All of our children, grandchildren, and great grand children, our prayer is that you will walk in your Godly heritage that has been laid before you and made available to you through the blood of Jesus and the word of this testimony.

I want to especially thank Pastor Don Wilkerson, who for the past 30 years has personally mentored Dianne and I and our family. His inspiration and support has been one of our greatest strengths.

Pastor Jimmy and Miriam Jack, our pastors, our friends, our mentors, and... our greatest fans. Lovingly cheering us on, always encouraging us to go to the next level and doing all in their power to help us accomplish what God put before us.

A special thanks to Cheryl Zehr, Director, Olive Press Messianic and Christian Publisher and her team for her patience and forebearance with us as we continually laid this book down because of life's interruptions. She never gave up on us and continued to encourage us to see it through to completion. Her team's expertise in editing and formatting and her guidance have resulted in a beautifully designed manuscript.

Last but not least, Pastor Joe Cedzich and his lovely, powerful wife Elaine, may she rest in peace, who are my spiritual parents. For over 30 years they interceded, prayed, cried, laughed and guided us through this journey of freedom in Christ. It was the doors of their church, "The Sheepgate" that the Jack and the Lloyd family went through and found the love and acceptance that would eventually lead to the founding of two of the most powerful ministries on Long Island. Long Island Teen Challenge and Long Island Citizens for Community Values.

ENDORSEMENTS

The Life of Reverend Bobby Lloyd as described and portrayed in this book is a miraculous example of how the Lord can rescue a person from the Pit of Hell and raise him to the heights of Heaven——Bobby is my son in the Lord. I am so proud of him May God bless and give hope to all who read this book.

Pastor Joseph Cedzich, Sheepgate Assembly

Pastor Joe and wife Elaine, "spiritual parents" to Bobby and Dianne. Elaine's steadfast prayers and love helped guide them through their tumultuous journey of restoration, from the day they met her until she went home to be with her Lord.

The *Black Knight* is a must read. Throughout the Bible, God often chose the most unlikely people to lead the way for His people. Moses, the one who cannot speak well, was God's mouthpiece. Paul, the one who killed the very people that he would eventually become. And so is Bobby Lloyd. Apparently doomed to life in prison, until God brought him out for His will, in order to fight the very fight that almost all others turned their back on.

When God ordains and people respond, life is good.

George Cote, Founder and Past Chairman of Board, LICCV, Managing Director Of Merrill Lynch, Vice President of Merrill Lynch Capital Markets, Independent Consultant for Capital Markets. Presently, happily retired

The Black Knight is riveting, inspiring and captivating. A powerful read testifying to the transformational and miraculous work of God. Bobby Lloyd's book will make you laugh, cry, and ultimately marvel in what God has done in a surrendered life. It is a compelling reminder that it does not matter how you start, it is how you finish.

Reverend Willie Ramos, Executive Director of Long Island Teen Challenge; Executive Director of Albany Teen Challenge; Associate Pastor of Freedom Chapel International Worship Center.

What a moving illustration of the grace of God, who promised that His plan for His children is for good, not for harm (Jer.29:11). Only God could turn the pain and darkness of those earlier years into a tribute to His faithfulness and a ministry that few would choose, but is so desperately needed. May Bobby's example challenge many to reach for and hold fast to the God who loves, rescues, heals and redeems.

Helen Adams, Founder S-Cap (Suffolk Citizens Against Pornography), Founder LICCV, Community Activist

Our hearts are racing, along with Black Knight, as if he were chasing an elusive train, pulling out of the station, filled with God's love, a Special girl, and hope. He has to run twice as fast and twice as hard to make it. The train is leaving behind a life of drugs, crime and violence. He makes it! Restoration of his soul, renewal and promise! A fast-paced read.

Marjorie Delmar, Retired Teacher, Oceanside High School, NY

"Bobby's life story from brutal criminal to guardian angel, is a living testament to the courage it takes to transform from the inside out; and that anyone can with the love of great people and the grace of God"

Ellen Cooperperson, CEO-Corporate Performance Consultants, Inc & President-CPC Family Business Division

9

For the years that I have known the man, Bobby Lloyd, it has been very blessed and encouraging to my life. He is a father, a husband, a preacher, a mentor, and one that loves Christ most of all. I believe his life's testimony and work, from where God has brought him from and where God is taking him to, will affect, minister, and transform the lives of many. If there's one book that should be read that will encourage the direction of your life and help you to hold on by faith in Jesus, it's this book.

Apostle Randy Brown, Ph.D.

Black Knight is a compelling heart pounding true story about the life and times of my friend and Brother Bobby Lloyd and his wife Dianne. *Black Knight* is in reality a story filled with the pathos and heart gripping reality of God's love and mercy, and how Bobby & Dianne triumphed over death by the power of faith that guides us through the worst of life's adversities.

"Diamond in the back sunroof top digging the scene...." Well some of us can finish those lyrics. However, just across the Long Island Sound in Norwalk Connecticut during the late 60's and 70's where I lived, I can hear Curtis Mayfield in the background. I can remember so many pimps and hustlers like my cousin Philly Red & classmate Blair "Steppin" Williams who never made it out of the game and never experienced the love and power and deliverance of a loving God.

As you read this book, you will be taken back to a time that only seems like a dream today because of the redemptive power of love. Cookie and I count it a blessing to know Pastor Bobby and Dianne, who are true Crusaders and Champions for Christ.

Visionary John & Cookie Harper
Harper International Ministries

10

FOREWORD

The *Black Knight* is a power story and testimony of an incredible life transformation. I have been an eye-witness to Bobby Lloyd being lifted by God's grace out of a hell hole of crime, violence, pornography, and drugs and into a new life in Christ. Amazingly Bobby went from being a drug lord to a servant of the Lord fighting against the purveyors of the very lifestyle he came out of. God has given him a great voice and platform now through the organization he and his wife Diana founded to spread the message that there is hope and freedom from addictions. I highly recommend this book. This story is going to help save someone else's life. Read it, pass it on.

Don Wilkerson, Founder, Teen Challenge, World Challenge and Global Teen Challenge; and Pastor Emeritus, Time Square Church.

FOREWORD BY JIMMY JACK

Bobby Lloyd has been one of the greatest influences in my life. As you read the *Black Knight*, every chapter of his redemptive story will impact your life as well. When I think of Bobby, there are multitudes of inspiring character traits that stand out, but three truly define who this man of God is: Provider, protector, and loyal friend.

When I was 6 years old, Bobby entered in to my family's life and became my older brother. As our entire family experienced violence and emotional pain (through my eight brothers and sisters tumultuous life styles, along with the consequences of my mother and father's involvement with the civil rights movement), Bobby was always there. He would come over late at night with his body guards, packing a gun to see how our family was doing. My father called him, "The Black Knight." When our house was robbed by drug addicts, Bobby was there. When my brothers or sisters were caught up in violent storms or were in need, Bobby was there.

Bobby truly was our family's "Black Knight" and that was *before* he gave his heart to Jesus. My sister Dianne, once a severe heroin addict, who became a passionate Christian, married Bobby. She saw something in him through the eyes of Christ that no one else saw. When Bobby entered a Christian drug and alcohol program, "Brooklyn Teen Challenge," his entire life was transformed through the power of Jesus Christ.

While living a deadly life style of crime and drug addiction, I visited a church where Bobby and his Teen Challenge quartet sang and testified of their new lives. I remember sitting in the front row listening them as my heart began to melt. A few weeks later, on November 4, 1984, I too entered Brooklyn Teen Challenge and changed my life forever. From that moment on, Bobby has been my partner, pastor, brother and armor-bearer in every ministry and mission we have established for the past 30 years. When my father called him, "The Black Knight," it was a prophetic role God would develop for Bobby's purpose to rescue, restore and redeem broken lives through the power of God.

Bobby is still packing a gun today; it's called the Bible. Bobby's life and mission, detailed in every page of this book, will bless your life as it has mine and thousands upon thousands of other people he has touched.

Jimmy Jack, President and Founder, Long Island Teen Challenge, Albany Teen Challenge, and Dominican Republic Teen Challenge; and Senior Pastor, Freedom Chapel International Worship Center.

TABLE OF CONTENTS

At the height of "success"

PROLOGUE

Traffic crept along—with all its starts and stops—over the Tri-Borough Bridge. The "city that never sleeps" seemed especially alive this particular night in April 1976.

The unforgiving New York traffic offered no special privileges to the flashy black coup carrying the three black men. To compound the misery of the trip, rain pelted the car, each new deluge eliciting a wave of brake lights in front of them.

Bobby Lloyd was not in a good mood. His right-hand man had been busted the night before carrying a parcel of *his* heroin. Now he was forced to return to his connection for more—no, not just his connection—his boss. Bobby was a foot soldier in a black crime family.

The congested bridge eventually dumped its inhabitants onto 125th Street in the heart of Harlem. The stylish Cadillac continued in the traffic flow through the business center, then south on Park Avenue and finally east on 117th Street. As the men rounded the corner, their eyes encountered a scene of utter contradiction, for here on this narrow street of burned out buildings and gutted tenements, sat the most flamboyant array of Cadillacs and Mercedes Benzes imaginable. [1]

The three pulled their own ritzy car in front of the nondescript building attracting all of the attention. Bobby slipped out of the driver's seat, leaving his two henchmen in custody of the car. There they stood, guns ready, for any perceived threat to their boss that these cruel streets might produce.

Bobby braved the deluge, ducking into a spacious room illuminated only by a few flickering lamps. Hands instinctively

---

[1] Today, 117th Street contains high-priced Brownstones and townhouses. In the mid-Seventies it had suffered the ravages of years of crime and neglect.

moved toward waistbands and chatter temporarily subsided at the opening of the door. Only a fool with a death wish would enter this building uninvited. This was the after-hours club of Nicky Barnes (recently made famous in the movie *An American Gangster*); he was "Mr. Untouchable" himself, the godfather of a multimillion-dollar drug empire and crime syndicate.

Bobby scanned the unpretentious room, noticing the usual array of hustlers, pimps, and pushers gathered around wooden tables, each of which offered its own jive-talking entertainer and small audience of amused listeners.

There he is, Bobby thought to himself, making his way to the back of the club. Leaning against the dingy wall was Solomon Glover, one of Nicky Barnes' lieutenants, who immediately led Bobby into a small room, hardly any bigger than a walk-in closet. "What's up man?" Solomon inquired, now that the two had privacy.

"My runner was busted by the feds last night," said Bobby matter-of-factly. "I need some more product."

"You want some more? Show me the money!" retorted his irritated boss.

"I'm broke, Solomon!" argued Bobby. "I gave it all up to you the last time I copped."

"Nigga' please! How I know you ain't makin' this up?" Solomon roared.

"Read the papers! It's right there on the back page!" Bobby was starting to get hot, his temper held in check by Solomon Glover's reputation as a heartless killer.

The clamor spilling from the over-sized closet brought an unexpected visitor. Nicky Barnes had presence—there was no denying that—an imposing aura that was only magnified in this tiny room. He possessed that rare combination of ruthlessness, street savvy and extraordinary intelligence that made him a larger-than-life icon to the people of Harlem.

"What's going on, Solomon?" There was no such thing as a simple question from him. To those addressed by the kingpin, every word carried with it the unspoken menace of someone possessing life-and-death power.

"The brother owes me money and he wants more product," Solomon whined.

"What about it?" Nicky asked, training steely eyes on Bobby.

"Look, my man got busted last night. We're low on cash. We need more product." His answers had the straightforward quality of someone telling the truth.

Turning back to Glover, Nicky asked, "How much does he owe you besides this?"

"He don't owe me nothin' else," Glover admitted.

"Are you crazy? You got guys who've owed you money for years and you're leaning on him over this? Give him what he wants! The package he lost? Forget it!" Barnes' verdict terminated the conversation.

Bobby emerged from the building with the bag in his pocket and a sense of relief that would prove short-lived. Little did he know that there were two federal agents sitting down the street in a government-issued Dodge, watching him through government-issued binoculars. Had they pulled his car over then—which they couldn't do without compromising their larger objective—they could have arrested the three men on assorted felony charges.

Nevertheless, within a week, the brash young criminal would be looking at life in prison. That inclement night began the downfall of Bobby Lloyd's criminal aspirations. He could never have guessed the fate that awaited him.

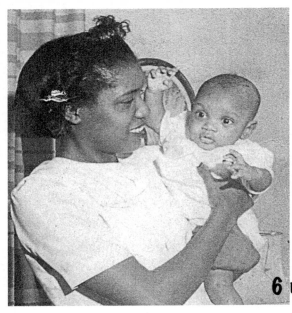
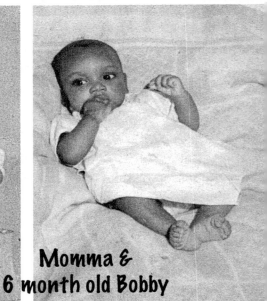

Momma &
6 month old Bobby

Aunt Eva

Little League

Setting the Stage

"What happened to *you*?" Bobby asked, looking at his battered younger brother. The 13-year-old was sporting a swollen lip and a shiner on his left eye.

"Some white dudes jumped me," Stevie moaned.

"I know your mouth. Whaddya say to 'em?" Bobby demanded, moving closer to get a better look at Stevie's bruised face.

"I didn't say nothin' that deserved this!" He retorted defensively.

Bobby couldn't argue with that! "Tell me who they are and I'll take care of it."

The next morning the 14-year-old brother was on a mission, arriving at South Side Junior High School with a sense of determination. Stevie struggled to keep up with his older brother as they searched the school for his assailants.

"That's one of 'em right there," he said, pointing at a tall white guy leaning up against a wall, talking to a pimple-faced girl.

Bobby marched up to the gangly teenager. "Yo, man!" And before the kid had a chance to run or fight, he punched him in the face, slamming his head into the wall with such force that it left a dent in it. The dazed kid simply slid down the wall and landed in a heap. Bobby kicked him in the stomach for good measure. "Don't you ever touch my brother again!" spat Bobby.

The two Lloyd brothers continued their search, finding the other kid behind the sprawling school, hanging out with some friends. When he noticed Bobby bearing down on him, he took off running, but Bobby was too quick for him. He caught up to him, grabbed him by the back of the shirt and yanked him to the pavement with so much force that the blow delivered a concussion.

Through this seemingly insignificant incident, Bobby Lloyd discovered two things about himself that day: he was a good fighter and he thoroughly enjoyed playing the part of savior. Yeah, he liked this new role... a lot. He was soon to discover other thrills as well.

****

Rockville Centre, a village in the township of Hempstead, in Nassau County, is situated on Long Island, three towns east of Queens. In the '50s and '60s it was a predominately white village. Actually, it was the ninth richest village per capita in the United States at that time. Affluent Rockville Centre had only one problem; it bordered the racially diverse town of Lakeview.

City council members decided to do something about Rockville Centre's community blemish and began drawing up the plans to build a towering wall creating a border clearly separating the two areas. They were well on their way to implementing their proposal when a fiery white lady named Adele Jack stepped in, outraged by the blatant racism involved. At the same time, Dr. Martin Luther King Jr. himself came to Rockville Centre to meet with her, along with some of the other black residents, including Earnestine Small, an activist in her own right. The whole plan was quickly abandoned when brought to the attention of state legislators in Albany.

It was within that small segregated black community on the edge of Rockville Centre, but still in the village—at 79 North Center Avenue to be exact—that Edward and Mary Lloyd raised their two boys, Bobby born in 1945 and Stevie the following year. The separated black area of run down houses was only about one mile long, with a few educated community-minded people like the Lloyd family. Bobby's parents, like most of the other black families in this area, were renters. Home ownership was rare. They rented a two-story Colonial home that still had some evidence of at one time having been very beautiful, but functionally, it lacked a lot.

Two kerosene heaters and a coal stove, which doubled as a cooking stove, provided the only source of heat to ward off the unforgiving New York winters. The boys' bedroom was so cold in the mornings that they could blow "smoke rings" with their breath. One morning, as he lay shivering under his covers, Bobby thought to himself, *When I grow up, I will never live like this—no matter what I have to do*!

Bobby's parents were unusual in their neighborhood because they both had steady jobs, were wise with their money, and stayed married all their lives. His father was a very big, powerful man who was kind, almost always smiling, and had an awesome sense of humor. In fact, he was affectionately known as "Radio" because he joked incessantly and you could never "shut him off." He loved partying, dancing, and flirting, but could also be very stern at times, and because of his size, no one messed with him. His reputation as a fierce fighter preceded him wherever he went. It was this reputation that Bobby would have to defend on the streets in his teen years. Mr. Lloyd worked as a car mechanic and was so strong he could remove an oil filter with his bare hand. He was known in the community as a man who kept his word.

Bobby's mother was a very thin, attractive woman who took good care of herself. She didn't finish school but was an avid reader. She was tough, rarely smiled, and did not show affection. She would always make a comment, usually something she didn't like about a person. It was her way of saying she liked them. She was often contrary, taking the opposite position of whatever was being discussed; she just liked to argue. Bobby's dad would often say she could argue with a lamppost. She seemed to love debating a person into an uproar. She worked as a cashier in the Grand Union in the neighborhood and by the time Bobby was 10, he was working there bagging groceries for his mother after school.

****

Bobby and Stevie and all the neighborhood boys, like other young boys of the '50s, derived enjoyment from simple boyhood pursuits such as playing ball, terrorizing girls, and throwing rocks at the trains that barreled through the edge of town. The neighborhood was like one big family. No one locked their doors. Parents discussed their plans together so much that if there was a new hot toy on the market at Christmas time, all the kids found that same hot item under their Christmas tree.

Bobby and Stevie's best friends were two brothers, Junior and Michael Paulson, who lived only a few houses down the street, Curtis Lundy who lived next door, and their cousin Lee. They ran in and out of each others' houses all day long, their moms hollering and giving them a good one with a switch when they got out of hand. The boys remained close friends all their lives.

The boys freely roamed the streets of their neighborhood as they played together, knowing where the boundaries were. The wealthy white neighborhood was only three blocks away, but it was forbidden territory to them. The unwritten rule was so deeply ingrained in them that they never dared to disobey it. Even the insatiable curiosity of their young minds did not overcome this unfair taboo.

Every now and then their run down, isolated black area was enlivened with some noteworthy event, such as when the train derailed at the station located right behind their homes, leaving crumpled box cars strewn all over the area surrounding the station. Another time a fire raged through the Coca-Cola plant, blowing up carbonated bottles by the thousands—very entertaining for boys to watch.

However, there were a few incidents that occurred in Bobby's boyhood that would have a much more profound impact on his future than any of these local catastrophes.

The first came at age six while he and Stevie were playing with Junior and Michael. The phone company had replaced a pole and left the old pole leaning up against the house. This was too much temptation for young boys. Oblivious to the impending danger, they decided to pull on the ropes that were wrapped around the huge telephone pole. To their amazement they were able to make it move! They kept tugging on the ropes, having great fun, until suddenly it came crashing down. It landed on Bobby, breaking both legs and fracturing his pelvis. His injuries were serious enough to require ongoing treatment for months. Because Bobby's family was "colored" they couldn't sue, but the phone company did pay the medical bills. On one of his follow-up visits, the orthopedic surgeon told the 6-year-old that his genitals needed to be examined "to make sure they're functioning properly." In doing so, the physician became aroused to the point of ejaculation. At that time, the young boy didn't understand any of this and just assumed it was part of the procedure. This incident repeated itself on each ensuing visit over the coming months.

Seven years later, Bobby began experiencing problems in his legs again and was forced to return to the doctor for another examination. By now he was a little savvier and this time he expected to be paid for his compliance. The doctor gave him $10, an exchange that would occur numerous times in the months ahead.

Not long after that first return visit he found a pornographic cartoon magazine lying in an alley. With wide-eyed fascination, the adolescent pored over the lurid images on its pages. He stashed his new treasure in the attic but would return to it many times over the following months.

The imagery he memorized in this magazine provided all the sex education young Bobby needed. Now he was anxious to experience the real thing. It happened soon enough when one of his friends told him he had been sexually involved with a neighborhood girl. Bobby immediately set about developing a scheme to have sex with her. He knew she had a penchant for ice cream, so one day he bought an ice cream cone and traded it for sexual favors.

These experiences, occurring during the early stages of puberty, had a devastating effect on him that would work itself out in hundreds of relationships in the years to come.

Home boys in 1955

Prom 1964

CHAPTER TWO

Building a Rep

As Bobby entered the teen years, he became more and more aware of the racial injustices against all those around him—injustices he and his friends were powerless to do anything about. This caused a subconscious anger to build up inside him. This anger quickly surfaced at the slightest provocation as we saw in his defense of his younger brother.

Bobby and Stevie were taught not to be violent. Whenever they exchanged blows at home, their mom whipped them both. Although his dad was not violent in the home he had a reputation as a street fighter and no one to be messed with. He was a steady, dependable man—who drank but wasn't an alcoholic, who was a womanizer but stayed married to their mom. However, he could be tough and stern. You didn't fool around with him in certain areas. He was a man of his word and demanded you be one too. If you didn't do what you said you were going to do, you would get a look, and you knew not to ever do that again. He would write you off in a second! These traits served well in his night job as a bouncer at a bar. This part of his character somewhat over-shadowed what their mom was telling them. If Bobby thought he or a friend was wronged, he didn't hesitate to use force to get even. He didn't see anything wrong in this. In his peer culture, defending yourself was the right thing to do.

One day he showed up for eighth-grade art class a couple minutes late, an infraction not lost to Mr. Bickle. Art lends itself to a free-flowing atmosphere and the young teen entered a classroom already bustling with activity and small talk.

Bobby made his way to his desk, along the wall near the door, flicking the ear of a freckled-faced kid as he strolled by. "Owwww," the boy whined, much to Bobby's enjoyment. Mr. Bickle was not amused. In fact, he was growing impatient with the young black kid's antics.

Bobby draped himself over his desk, his face coming to a halt no more than a foot away from the blond girl who sat next to him. Debbie thought Bobby was refreshingly entertaining and did not mind this incursion upon her space. He immediately started offering commentary on some of the other students, which quickly brought the girl to laughter.

Just as quickly, the smile left Debbie's face, as she noticed Mr. Bickle marching down the aisle of seats toward them. "Get off that desk and leave that girl alone!" barked the irritated teacher.

Even at this young age, Bobby had an exceptional ability to remain calm inside, no matter what might confront him. In this particular instance, he simply ignored the teacher. "Now where was I before I was so rudely..."

The red-faced teacher grabbed Bobby by the back of the collar and, in one grand expenditure of middle-aged energy, slung the insubordinate teenager into the wall.

The powerfully built boy bounced off the wall and came right back at the startled teacher. Grabbing him by the front of his shirt, Bobby turned him around, slammed him into the same spot on the wall, yanked him out the door and pushed him down the stairway. The art teacher tumbled all the way down with Bobby hot in pursuit. As he landed at the bottom, the teenager was on him pounding his face with his fists. Other students quickly pulled him off the overwhelmed man before any more damage was done.

Mr. Bickle picked himself up off the floor. "I'll have you kicked out of school for this!" he screamed hysterically. As it turned out, the principal tried to expel Bobby until parents of some of the other kids complained that the teacher brought it on himself by grabbing the youngster.

At this point, Bobby wasn't setting out to build a "rep" as a bad dude; he just reacted to incidents when they came his way—just doing what he thought he had to do to survive. One such situation happened the following year—1961—in Bobby's freshman year at South Side High School.

It occurred during their annual basketball humiliation at the hands of arch-rival Kerry High. South Side High School of Rockville Centre was mostly made up of smart kids from rich families, while the kids from Kerry came from a middle class area. Every year the two basketball teams met, and every year South Side was hammered.

Bobby wasn't a great basketball fan, but chose to go this time. On the way to the game he picked up his two close friends—Willie and Eddie. Willie grew up in the South and had a drawl that caused his sentences to linger on indefinitely. Eddie was the polar opposite of his southern friend. He styled himself as some kind of intellectual and was always philosophizing about something or other, even if he didn't know what he was talking about. Bobby liked both of the boys and they liked him, too.

Arriving at the game, the trio entered the raucous gymnasium as the two teams were still practicing at opposite ends of the court. It was an exhilarating experience for the young teens—the noise, the anticipation, even the pungent smell of sweat that always seemed to hover thickly in such places.

The boys dutifully went directly to the Rockville side of the gym. It was a common understanding that the home team sat on their side of the court and the visitors on the other—never the twain to meet.

"Nice shot, number 24!" came a voice of sarcasm after a South Side player missed a free throw. "You're gonna be a big help today—to Kerry!" His commentary set off a chorus of laughter from the other Kerry High boys surrounding him.

Bobby probably wouldn't have thought much about this kind of trash talking *if it came from the Kerry side of the gym.* But this catcalling was coming from above him.

"Look at those dudes!" Bobby exclaimed to his friends. "What do they think they're doin' on our side of the gym? They actin' like they own the place!" It was obvious to him that these kids were purposely disrespecting South Side.

Bobby started up the bleachers, his two buddies right on his heels. "Excuse me," said Bobby, interrupting the loudmouth. "Why don't you guys go over to your side of the gym?" Bobby seemed to be oblivious to the fact that these white boys were older and bigger than he.

"Yeah? And who's gonna make us?" The leader sneered. "You and your mama?" No sooner had the other kids started to laugh before Bobby plunged into their midst. In one fast motion, he grabbed the loudmouth by his shirt and threw him right off the top of the bleachers. Willie and Eddie started pummeling two of the other teens, while Bobby pounced on the fourth one. Eventually, some teachers made it to the top of the bleachers and rescued the bloodied Kerry students.

The three young black kids didn't have long to revel in their newly found notoriety, for the next day the principal called a special meeting in the gymnasium with all the boys of the school. The crowd was more boisterous than usual, but the clamor died down as the principal walked to the front of the stands. "Yesterday, there was a terrible display of unsportsmanlike conduct here," he said gravely. "We really disrespected ourselves."

As he continued his speech, Bobby became increasingly heated, until his inner agitation overcame all common sense. "Excuse me," he blurted out. "Are we allowed to speak or are you gonna go on talkin' about somethin' you don't know nothin' about? You weren't even here!"

Dead silence descended upon the entire gym.

"I'm not surprised you were at the bottom of this, Lloyd," the academic bureaucrat retorted weakly. He had been warned by his associates at the junior high school about Bobby.

Brushing his comment aside, Bobby persisted. "You wanna talk about respect? You *earn* respect. What they deserved was a beatin' and that's just what they got! I asked those guys to sit on their side and one of them smarted off to me so I threw him off the bleachers. And you know what? I'd do it again!" At that, the entire gymnasium erupted in applause and cheers. The school had a new hero and he was a mere freshman.

Later, the principal met with Bobby. "Listen, what you did yesterday was wrong, but I agree with you: respect is something you earn," the humbled principal told him. "Today, you earned my respect."

Yes, he earned the principal's respect but, much more importantly to him, his reputation as someone you don't mess with was now etched in the minds of every kid in that school.

**Young bloods
1961**

Pictured:
Bobby with his brother, Stevie, and Ernest (Tu Baby)

𝔗𝔥𝔢 𝔇𝔲𝔡𝔢𝔰 𝔉𝔯𝔬𝔪 𝔔𝔲𝔢𝔢𝔫𝔰

Gladys was literally "the girl next door." Bobby wasn't interested in her, but Benny Boy was. And that's how the two met.

As someone who didn't mind a fight, Bobby respected strength. So the first time he saw Benny Boy he wasn't very impressed. *That dude can't weigh more than 120 pounds*, Bobby mused to himself.

It was true. Benny Boy didn't look very intimidating. But Bobby gained a whole new admiration for his newfound friend the first time he saw him fight. It all started when Melvin, a stocky boy with light brown skin, began mouthing off to Benny down at the park. Benny Boy hit him one time and Melvin dropped to the ground as if he had just been shot dead. Looking down at his dark-skinned comrade, Bobby exclaimed, "Man, you knocked him clean out, Benny!"

Yes, Benny's looks were clearly deceiving. Not only was he a trained boxer, but he had been blessed in life with lightning speed. He could hit an opponent three times before the poor sap even knew what had happened. And his punches weren't the light slaps one might expect from a skinny guy; his oversized hands landed with punishing force. The truth is that most of his fights ended in one-punch knockouts.

The only thing he could do faster than throw punches was talk. He spoke so fast that, unless you were used to being around him, you could hardly make out what he was saying. White people? Forget it; they didn't understand *anything* he said.

Although he was a few years older than Bobby, the two soon became fast friends, and it wasn't long before he was teaching his younger buddy how to box down at the local gym. While Bobby was happy to learn some moves, he lacked the discipline to become a legitimate boxer.

In Bobby's area, on Long Island, only the strong boys survived. You didn't let people walk over you. They didn't have gangs like Blood or Crips. It was just towns against towns or villages against villages and it wasn't ongoing. When fights did break out, it was usually over a girl. Before you knew it, the towns were at "war" for awhile with each other. The violence was mostly just from brute force. Up to this point, no weapons were involved.

One day Benny Boy showed up at Bobby's house. "Bobby-I-think-Gladys-down-at-movie-with-some-dudes-from-Queens," he machine-gunned. "I-need-some-help." Gladys was a decent girl, but she had one great defect in life: she was a flirt and loved receiving attention from different guys.

"Sure, no problem."

The two friends paid for their tickets and entered the darkened theater. They walked straight down to the front of the cinema and began looking back up into the crowd of movie goers, straining to find the wayward girl and her temporary source of affection. "Bobby, they're-up-on-the-second-floor-over-by-that-rail!"

The two teenagers made their way up the stairs and found Gladys cuddled up with some stranger. "Gladys, come-on-out-here," said Benny. "I-need-to-talk-to-ya'."

"Yo, man," the guy said, tightening his arm around the 17-year-old girl. "She with me. Whatcha gonna do about it?" He smirked with utter disdain for his skinny rival.

By now people around them were becoming more interested in their drama than the predictable storyline on the screen.

Benny Boy didn't see any purpose in discussing the matter. He swung at the black dude, his punch bouncing off his head. When the stranger jumped out of his seat, Bobby grabbed him and threw him right over the handrail. He then sprinted down the stairway after him, pounding him in the face before he could recover.

By now security officers had shown up. Bobby and Benny knew the theater and made their escape out the back door.

A couple of days later, Benny Boy was visiting Bobby at his house when four "souped-up" cars pulled up in front of Gladys' house. About twenty young black men emerged from the vehicles wearing matching silk bandanas and hats tilted to the side that marked them as members of a legitimate gang.

"Benny, this don't look good. I'm goin' for some help!" At that, Bobby snuck across the street to a friend's house and told him to round up some of the Rockville group.

There was a store across the street where people hung out and a park nearby where they all played ball. So putting together a group was not a problem, especially since it was Saturday. Within minutes, the menacing gang was crowding around Bobby and Benny Boy. Gladys' new boyfriend still looked battered from the beating he had received from Bobby and was clearly intent on revenge.

The two friends knew help was on the way and did their best to stall the situation without losing face. As Bobby scanned the crowd, he saw something of much greater concern than the angry boyfriend. A slim guy with a fierce look on his face was standing a few feet away, his trench coat bulging noticeably on the right side. *That looks like a sawed-off shotgun*, he thought to himself. *I'm gonna get as close to him as possible and if anything goes down, I'm gonna hit that dude as hard as I can and get that gun!*

As the intruders were milling around, Bobby started cautiously maneuvering himself toward the dude with the shotgun. Just as he reached his proximity—and much to his relief—four carloads of Rockville "brothers" careened around the corner, one after another, pulling up right in front of the hostile crowd. They jumped out of the cars and rushed behind Benny.

Now there were nearly fifty black guys squared off on the dead-end street. The fierce-looking man with the shotgun started becoming very agitated and trying to provoke his buddies to get a fight started. "I'll kill anyone here!" he screamed. It was becoming increasingly clear to Bobby that he was high on something—probably speedballs by the unstable way he was acting—and that he was liable to do anything.

This is gonna turn into a bloodbath, Bobby thought to himself. *I gotta hit him now!* Just as he positioned himself to coldcock the agitator, the guy's brother came over and began calming him down. "Another day, another time," he said reassuringly to his younger sibling. "Another day, another time."

At that, the gang from Queens started easing away from the Rockville crew. "We'll finish this later!" one of them said as they piled back into their cars. Benny and the rest of his friends quietly stood their ground as the four cars of intruders backed down the street and took off.

Perhaps the entire incident would have blown over, if Bobby hadn't foolishly showed up in Queens not more than a week later.

Willie had met a couple of girls who happened to live there and arranged for him and Bobby to come over for a visit. They jumped on a bus that day and made the short jaunt over to Queens. The careless pair stepped off the bus onto the crowded sidewalk, when Bobby noticed a dozen members of the same gang standing not more than ten yards away. "Hey, I know you!" one of them yelled.

"Run!" Bobby shouted to Willie and the two took off down the street with the angry gang hot on their trail. They ran for all they were worth that day, dodging pedestrians and oncoming cars alike, as they scrambled to escape the pursuing posse.

The two reached a corner. Bobby's feet nearly slid out from under him, as he twisted his body to make the turn. Just then, another bus pulled up right in front of them—as if specially sent by Heaven itself. The frightened teenagers scampered through the door, huffing and puffing. "Man, please take off!" Willie pleaded, his southern drawl completely absent. "Those dudes are gonna kill us!"

Apparently the driver was no stranger to the daily dramas of New York street life. "No problem," he said. "I know the neighborhood!" With that, he slammed the door shut with a hiss and hurtled his urban tank into the flow of traffic. The gasping gang reached the bus, only to be treated with a blast of black smoke.

Five blocks later the thankful teenagers—giggling with nervous relief—jumped off the bus and made their way back to Rockville Centre. The quick thinking of that driver very well could have spared the two from being stomped to death on a busy and uncaring street in downtown Queens.

Apparently the Queens gang saw their visit as an affront. Two days later they sent word that they would be over that night "to get their pound of flesh." The Rockville boys were waiting, but were surprised when 35 gang members showed up. They were outnumbered nearly two-to-one.

There was no talk this time. As soon as they emerged from their cars the two groups began fighting, using baseball bats, knives, and chains. Just as Bobby slashed one kid in the neck with his knife, someone else hit him in the back with a pipe.

Meanwhile, police cruisers descended on the brawl from every direction. To their surprise, the gangbangers quit fighting each other and turned their fury upon the cops. At one point, one of the guys from Queens hit an officer with a baseball bat, sending him sprawling on the blacktop. Bobby recognized the cop, a man who was known for his fairness. As the kid was about to slam the bat down on the frightened officer's head, Bobby yanked him backwards, giving the policeman a chance to scramble back to his feet.

As suddenly as they had arrived, the gang departed. The incident provided Bobby another opportunity to fulfill his favorite roles as fighter and savior.

CHAPTER FOUR

Fast and Furious

Fred Sanford (i.e., the '70s sitcom *Sanford and Son*) and his salvage operation is the best description one could offer to define Mr. Bill and his auto body shop, which happened to be located around the corner from the Lloyd home. Mr. Bill and his nephew Charles didn't ever get much car work done—although there always seemed to be one squeezed into their small, cluttered garage. To Bobby, the comical pair seemed to spend all their time talking—a never-ending source of entertainment to a bored 15-year-old.

One Saturday afternoon, a rich kid from "Jew Hill," as it was called then, arrived in his sparkling blue Corvette Stingray, which had sustained some minor front-end damage. It was unfortunate timing on this young man's part for Bill and Charles were well on their way to "tying one on." As soon as the Jewish boy left, the pair decided to head for the Bee Hive, the local black bar. "Watch the shop," Bill slurred to Bobby.

"No problem, Mr. Bill," answered the eager teenager. Bobby couldn't believe his luck! He watched the two stagger down the street, laughing, cussing and carrying on. As soon as the cavorting twosome were out of sight, Bobby jumped in the sports car and began revving its powerful engine.

He pushed the clutch to the floor and eased the transmission into reverse—at least what he thought was reverse—and popped the clutch, expecting to lay down a nice patch of rubber as he made a dramatic, James Bond-style exit from the garage. To his utter astonishment, the car violently lurched forward instead, right into the rear wall of the shop! He jumped out of the car to check the damage. The front end had already been wrecked so he figured his drunken boss wouldn't notice that—but the rear wall had been pushed two inches off the foundation. *Oh no!* Bobby thought to himself. *How am I gonna fix that?*

He ran around the back of the shack to see what could be done. *I'll just do the same thing from the other side*, he announced to himself. So he started up one of the old heaps that served as perpetual landmarks to the establishment and rammed it right into the back of the garage. And what do you know but the wall slid right back into place! Bobby congratulated himself over his quick thinking and Mr. Bill was never the wiser for it.

Unfortunately, it soon became obvious that the young teen hadn't learned his lesson when another white guy brought his '55 Chevy in for a little work on the right rear fender. Mr. Bill wasn't around and the conniver saw an opportunity to get the work done on the cheap. "Hey, you do body work?"

"Absolutely," Bobby replied, with a ridiculous amount of confidence.

"I'll tell you what," the stranger continued. "You patch up this dent by this afternoon and there's a twenty dollar bill in it for you."

"You got it," said Bobby. The man then got in his wife's car and drove off.

It didn't take Bobby two minutes before he was behind the wheel of that hotrod, barreling down the street. He picked up Benny, Willie, and Eddie, and the gang spent the rest of the afternoon driving around Rockville Centre. The only problem was that he didn't know how to drive a stick shift. By the time he made it back to the garage, a terrible burning smell filled the car.

Undaunted, he went right to work on the fender, finishing it up minutes before the man returned. The miser paid Bobby his cut-rate price and got in his hotrod. He was pretty pleased with his savings until he started it up and tried backing out of the shop. It was then he noticed the clutch was slipping terribly. Suddenly, it all became clear to him. *That punk was out joyriding in my car!* He gave Bobby a piece of his mind, promising to return the next day. Bobby just shrugged him off.

True to his word, he showed up the following morning, complaining to Mr. Bill. "Listen, you gave him the car and that's on you!" Bill responded. "I don't wanna hear nothin' about it. You brought this on yourself by trying to get slick on me. Besides, you better leave that boy alone 'cause he'll hurt ya."

****

Bobby sincerely enjoyed working on vehicles, but hotrods were his greatest source of fascination. And it was this love for fast cars that brought him into an unlikely friendship with a couple of "square" white guys his age. The first was Russell Jack, the oldest of the nine children of Alex and Adele Jack—the civil rights lady. Mr. Jack was an administrator in athletics. They lived right across the way on the white side of town. The other guy was an Italian kid named Richie who also lived nearby.

By the time they were seventeen, the three guys all had their own hotrods. Bobby owned a '55 Chevy, Russell tooled around in a '57 Ford, and Richie had a '55 Thunderbird. All three cars had reworked engines. All three cars could flat out fly.

One particular night, the three were fooling around in Russell's garage. Richie and Bobby decided to drive around in the T'bird. No one would expect a stylish car like this to be sporting a hot 348 Chevy engine.

The two were cruising on Sunrise Highway when a couple of white guys in a Mustang pulled alongside them. "Hey, you wanna race?" yelled the driver.

"Let's do it!" responded Bobby from the passenger's seat.

The two cars pulled to a stop at a red light, gunning their engines. Sunrise Highway had somehow become dubbed the local drag strip, in spite of the fact that it was a busy thoroughfare running right through Rockville Centre. Both drivers revved their engines and took off as soon as the light changed.

The other guy got the jump on Richie, but it took less than two seconds for the T'bird to kick into gear before it screamed past the Mustang. Richie and Bobby were gloating as their defeated opponents pulled up alongside them at the next light.

The white boy was humiliated and angry. "Listen, this is just my cruising car, but I've got another one at home that can beat that thing you're driving. You follow me to my house and we'll race for a hundred bucks," he challenged.

"Alright," Richie agreed.

The two Rockville boys followed the Mustang into Garden City and, sure enough, the guy pulled out of his garage with a different Mustang—this one fire engine red. Unbeknownst to them, a carload of the guy's friends followed the two cars back to Rockville Centre.

Once again they squared off and once again they blew past the other guy's car. When they got a ways down the road, Richie pulled over along the shoulder of the road. Just as they were getting out of the Thunderbird, the third car pulled up behind their friends. Five guys got out of the two cars and approached the two.

"Okay, man," said Bobby. "Where's our money?"

The driver said, "I got yer money," and hit Bobby right in the mouth. Bobby slammed him down on the hood of the car and the fight was on. The problem was that Richie had taken off running, leaving Bobby to fend for himself. Two of the guys from the third car grabbed him from behind. He still managed to kick one of them before falling under a rain of blows. The sore loser and his friends walked off laughing, leaving Bobby lying on the side of the road, gasping for breath.

There was one small detail they hadn't considered: Bobby knew where the guy lived. And he was angry, very angry. Not only had they stiffed him for a hundred bucks, but five of them had jumped him as well.

He drove Richie's car back to his neighborhood and rounded up Benny, Willie, Eddie, Meat, Russell Jack, and three carloads of other friends. It only took a few minutes to drive to Garden City, but it took 45 minutes before they found the house. "There's that Mustang!" Bobby exclaimed.

Nineteen black guys burst through the front door of the house. To their surprise, they had walked right into the middle of a family reunion. Bobby was too angry to care, grabbing the main perpetrator and dragging him outside. While he beat down the cheater, his friends calmly stood guard.

Had the guy's family left well enough alone, it would have ended at that. But they jumped up and started yelling at the intruders. One of them made the mistake of yelling, "You niggers get outta here!" That was music to their ears because now everyone was an open target. The brothers attacked the white males who were there, giving every one of them a thorough beating.

Once again Bobby Lloyd resolved conflict by dishing out physical punishment. It was becoming a way of life for him and his friends.

**Bobby's girls
Dawn and Monique, Cheryl's daughters
and Paula, Ulamay's daughter**

CHAPTER FIVE

The Hempstead Rumble

It all started over Ulamay, a buxom, dark-complexioned beauty who lived in the Campbell Park projects. This jungle of rundown apartment buildings was situated smack dab in the middle of Hempstead, the small city just north of Rockville Centre. [Both Rockville Centre and Hempstead "villages" are located in Hempstead Township in Nassau County.]

Ulamay became Bobby's main girlfriend during his sophomore year of high school. Once a week or so, he, Willie, and Eddie would cut school, catch a bus to Hempstead and visit Uly (Ulamay's nick name) and a couple of her girlfriends. Eddie had somehow gotten his hands on a chauffeur's license claiming he was 18 years old. So if they were fortunate enough to have some cash, the trio would stop by the corner liquor store on the way over and pick up a couple bottles of Thunderbird. The three couples would have a middle-of-the-day party before drifting into various bedrooms for a youthful round of sexual frenzy.

Ula eventually got pregnant and gave birth to a little girl she named Paula. But once she started becoming large with child, Bobby lost interest in her. In fact, it was at this time he had his eye on a bronze beauty from his hometown, Cheryl, with whom he would later sire two daughters, Monique and Dawn.

They say that hell hath no fury like a woman scorned. Well, Ula was none too happy with Bobby when he started ignoring her, and she decided a dose of revenge was in order. One of her neighbors was Reginald Wilson, who had a reputation of being a punishing fighter.

Ula sauntered up to him in front of his apartment one morning. "Reggie," she purred in his ear. "Did you know that Bobby Lloyd been tellin' everyone he's gonna do some serious damage to you?" Reginald's eyes narrowed as he listened.

"Nobody gonna talk about me like that," he announced to her as he walked away. Reginald immediately decided to teach Bobby a lesson. *I ain't goin' down to Rockville*, he thought to himself. *He'll be comin' back and when he shows up here? I'll be waitin'!*

As Ula well knew, Bobby was bringing her some cash for the baby that very day. Later that afternoon, he pulled his '55 Chevy into the projects, avoiding the numerous potholes dotting the parking lot. He had already been drinking and was being unusually careless.

As he trudged along to Ula's apartment, Reginald Wilson and two other brothers stepped out of a doorway, just in front of him. Bobby sensed that something was wrong, but he was just buzzed enough to put on a brave face. "How's it goin', Reginald?" he asked the guy who he knew mainly by reputation.

Reginald brushed aside his pleasantries. "Hey, man, I hear you wanna piece of me!" he growled. Bobby was a tough fighter, but even in his tipsy condition he had the sense enough to know when he was in over his head. Reginald was 6 feet 1 inch tall, with a body that looked like it had been hand chiseled. He was definitely *not* someone you were looking to fight for fun and pleasure.

"Man, where'd this come from?" Bobby asked, as he approached the three young toughs. "I got no beef with you."

"I can't be havin' people throwin' my name around!" came the hard answer. And before Bobby even had a chance to respond, Reginald punched him hard in the side of his face. The punch came with such force that the 22 pistol tucked in Bobby's waistband soared into the bushes. Amazingly, Reginald didn't notice. Bobby picked himself up off the sidewalk and charged his nemesis. Reginald simply stepped to his right and walloped him again. This time the defeated man thought better of getting up. "Next time you talk about me you won't get off so easy," Reginald snapped as he and his smiling friends casually walked away. Later on that night Bobby went back and found his gun.

****

"Man, you're a mess!" exclaimed Billy. "What happened?" It had only taken two Reginald Wilson punches to completely swell the left side of Bobby's face.

"I was takin' some money over to Ula today and Reginald Wilson jumped me!"

"We ain't gonna put up with that! Come on. Let's go get the boys!"

When there was trouble, Billy was definitely the brother you wanted on your side. He was angry in life; that's all there was to it. Even in the best of times his words had an edge—a combative and hostile edge. He was only about 5 feet 6 inches tall, but he was as solid as a brick wall and a vicious, knife-toting street fighter.

Where did they go first? Right to George's house. Their friend George was big: 6 feet 5 inches tall, weighing nearly 280 pounds. His voice was deep and gravelly, as though talking was a painful experience. George didn't say much, but when he did speak, he commanded instant respect. He was definitely an intimidating presence.

The three piled into George's '63 Thunderbird, picked up fast-talkin' Benny Boy, and drove up Peninsula Boulevard, right into the heart of Hempstead. They cruised through the Campbell Park projects failing to find Reginald. As they eased the man's luxury ride out of the parking lot, Bobby spotted one of the guys. "There's one!" he cried, pointing at a group of guys standing around in the park, about a hundred yards away.

At that, Billy and Bobby both pulled out their pieces and started sparking rounds at the group. There must have been ten brothers there and they all started diving for cover. One of them crumpled to the ground.

Sitting off to the side in a white convertible was another guy they hadn't noticed. He grabbed a .22 rifle from under his seat and started firing back, a bullet whizzing by Billy's ear before slamming into the mirror. Shards of glass sprayed the foursome.

George gunned the T'bird and they raced away, laughing with excitement over the exchange.

"Man, did you guys see Bobby?" exclaimed Benny. "He was actin' like Wyatt Earp shootin' up the O-K Corral!"

****

Two days later, Bobby was sitting in front of the house of his childhood buddies Junior and Michael, talking to their cousin Preston who lived with them, when he noticed an older model Cadillac turn onto his block. It was creeping along slowly when suddenly, as if the occupants had just noticed the trio sitting there, the old Caddie came barreling toward them. "Look out!" Bobby yelled to his friends. But the speeding car was on them before they could get away.

The brother on the passenger side threw a Molotov cocktail out the window right at them. Fortunately it fell short, hitting the curb with an explosion, its fiery contents shooting ten feet across the sidewalk and up into the yard.

Bobby jumped up, pulling his two pearl-handled revolvers out of his waistband and started "popping caps" at the fleeing assailants. The driver must have gotten hit because the Caddie lurched to a stop at the end of the block, and one of the passengers ran around and jumped into the driver's seat.

****

This feud between the Rockville and Hempstead gangs continued for the next year. Sometimes the gangs would run into each other at a party, at which time a fight would immediately break out. Other times, some unfortunate victim would be caught alone by the opposing gang and receive a thorough beating.

One evening Bobby, Billy, Willie, and Eddie decided to drive by Hempstead Park. This time they were in Eddie's '58 Chevy. He eased his ride up to the edge of the park and shut the motor off. They could see the Hempstead boys in their usual spot out in the park, drinking and cutting up. The four brothers emerged from the Chevy and just stood there trying to decide what to do.

Suddenly, Eddie impulsively yelled out, "Hey, here's Bobby Lloyd!" Bobby looked at him like he had lost his mind; they were, after all, vastly outnumbered and on enemy turf.

The other gang instantly ceased their antics and began peering at the four intruders. Perhaps they suspected an ambush or maybe they just didn't believe him. In any event, they hesitatingly started ambling toward the group of strangers.

Facing insurmountable odds, the Rockville brothers knew it was time to hightail it out of there. As they piled back into the Chevy, one of the Hempstead boys shouted, "It *is* Bobby

Lloyd!" The nine ruffians now broke into a full sprint toward the intruders' car.

Eddie fumbled with the key and jammed it into the ignition switch. To their utter horror, as he turned the key the starter cranked but the engine wouldn't respond! On and on the starter groaned as the angry mob flew toward them. Every eye darted back and forth from the key to the charging gang; every mind frantically trying to figure out how they would get out of this predicament. As the gang descended upon the unresponsive car, the engine suddenly roared to life. Eddie gunned it, speeding out of the parking lot and back onto the street.

It was a missed opportunity for Hempstead and a very close call for Rockville Centre. There would be plenty more for young Bobby Lloyd.

High School Graduation
1964

Mr. and Mrs.
Lloyd Sr.

CHAPTER SIX

In Trouble with the Man

"You're supposed to be home by ten!" Bobby's father gave him a stern look one night when he was a few minutes late.

"I can come home any time I want!" Bobby retorted. "Who are you to tell me what to do? You're getting old." That was all it took. His dad towered over him, put his huge hands around the teen's neck, lifted him by the chin and back of his head, and carried him up the stairs. Bobby never challenged his father again.

"Bobby, come down here, now!" his father boomed from down in the living room on another evening.

The 16-year-old shuffled down the stairway to see what the trouble was. To his surprise, a white police officer was standing just inside the front door.

"Listen, we just arrested a kid named Billy who said he gave you the gun he stole from the school today," said the policeman, getting right to the point. "Just give us the gun and we won't arrest you," he assured the teenager. "We just want that gun back."

"I don't got no gun," Bobby lied.

"Son, if you have this gun, you need to give it to him," said his father.

"I ain't got no gun," Bobby insisted, nervously shuffling his foot across the worn, wooden floorboards.

"Bobby, if you got this gun, you need to give it to him," his father repeated, standing up. "You gotta obey the law, son."

Bobby hesitated as he weighed his father's words. It was against his better judgment, but he decided to do what his father said. "Okay." He walked back up the stairs to his bedroom and retrieved the revolver. "Here you go," he said, handing it to the cop.

"Okay, but I've got to arrest you."

I will never trust the word of a cop again! Bobby fumed to himself, as he rode in the back of the squad car to the Nassau County Sheriff's Station. That was the first time Bobby Lloyd was arrested.

****

A couple of years later, he and Willie were cruising around in Bobby's '55 Chevy. They ended up in Baldwin, a predominately white town a few miles from Rockville Centre. The car had been running poorly all evening, when suddenly it backfired, spit, coughed, and died right on Merrick road. Bobby pulled it to the curb in front of a local tavern.

"Wait here," Bobby told his friend. "I'll go inside and call Mr. Bill."

The black teenager entered the pub and walked up to the counter to ask the bartender for some change. "Say, nigger!" yelled some belligerent white man, sitting at the other end of the bar. Without the slightest hesitation, Bobby marched right up to the drunk and hit him so hard he flew off his barstool and landed on the floor. The guy's friend on the next stool started to stand up and Bobby knocked him out with one punch, too. As that happened, another guy grabbed him from behind. Bobby snatched a beer bottle sitting on the counter, spun around and cracked him over the head. By now he was hot. He grabbed a barstool and slammed it over the head of a fourth man, who, by this point, wasn't interested in being involved. Within seconds, all four men were laid out on the floor bleeding.

In the meantime, the bartender had called the police. Bobby left the pub before the cops arrived and sat out front in Eddie's stalled car. He wasn't worried because, as far as he was concerned, he hadn't done anything wrong.

To his surprise, the police arrested *him* when they showed up a few minutes later. He couldn't believe it! Once again, he made the trip to the Nassau County Jail in Mineola, where he was booked for assault with a deadly weapon.

Two days later, he stood before the judge at his arraignment. The judge looked at the 18-year-old black kid. Then he eyed the four grown white men. "What's going on here?" he asked, turning his gaze to the assistant district attorney.

"Well, your honor, this kid attacked these men," responded the prosecutor.

"You mean to tell me that these four men are pressing charges against this one kid?" he asked incredulously. Turning now to Bobby, he said, "Son, tell me exactly what happened."

"Sir, our car broke down and I went into this bar to call for help. That man there," pointing to the guy nearest him, "called me a nigger. So I got angry and we got into a fight. His buddies tried to jump me, so I did what I had to do to defend myself." His story wasn't entirely true, but it was believable enough to the judge.

The judge turned back to the district attorney. "Case dismissed," he said pointedly. "I want this arrest expunged off this young man's record. Don't ever bring a case like this into my courtroom again!"

****

By this point, Bobby was starting to hang out at bars himself. For the most part, the Bee Hive was a hangout for older guys, but there were occasions when Bobby and his friends would spend time there too.

One particular Saturday night, a bunch of young people were at the end of the bar near the front door. They were all drinking and cutting up. "Hey, why don't we go over to West Side?" asked Willie, in his southern drawl, referring to another bar. "There's more room o'er there."

So the whole bunch piled into two cars—one of which was Bobby's—and they drove over to the other tavern. Sheila, one of the girls in the party, had been drinking fairly heavily. Maybe it was riding in the back seat that brought it on, but she ended up throwing up in the back of his '55 Chevy. Bobby was disgusted, but he wasn't going to let it ruin his fun. They drove on over to the other bar and continued their party.

The group melted into a larger crowd of young people there and Sheila ended up leaving the pub with some other guys.

Bobby stayed for several hours and finally started driving home. All of the sudden, a police cruiser pulled in behind him. *Oh, man*, he sighed. *I hope they don't pull me over!* Sure enough, a couple of blocks further the flashing lights started spinning and Bobby maneuvered his Chevy to the curb.

"What's the problem, officer?" Bobby inquired of the patrolman through his window.

"You Bobby Lloyd?" the cop asked.

"Yes, I am."

"Please step out of the car." When Bobby got out of his car, the officer handcuffed him. "You're wanted for questioning at headquarters about some girl who was raped."

Once again, Bobby took the ride down to the Nassau County police station. When he arrived, he noticed Sheila sitting with a female officer on one of the benches.

"What's this all about?!" Bobby demanded. "This is crazy!" He was getting very agitated by now, as the officer led him to a back room.

"This girl says she was in your car and you raped her," answered the officer.

"Yeah, a bunch of us were driving around," he retorted. "That girl got so drunk she threw up in the back of my car. That's the last I saw of her. She went off with some other dudes."

Just then a detective who knew Bobby happened by. "What are you doing in here, Bobby?"

"Man, they're trying to say I raped this girl. I keep tryin' to tell these guys that I didn't rape nobody!"

The investigator pulled the arresting officers to the side. "Listen, I know this guy. He's not the type to rape someone. Let me go talk to this girl."

The detective went out front and approached Sheila. "Miss, I'm Detective Martin. Are you sure that this guy Bobby Lloyd raped you?" he asked, leaning closer to her.

By now the girl was sobering up and starting to have second thoughts. "Well, uh, the first face I remembered when I woke up in the hospital was Bobby's. I guess I just assumed he was the one," she said weakly. "But now that I think about it, I think it was some guys I met at the West Side bar.

**The Jack Family
1958**

**March on
Washington
in 1963**

**Mr & Mrs Jack
1966**

**Mr. Jack
1978**

CHAPTER SEVEN

The Family Protector

"Hey nigger!"

Bobby, who was casually walking down the sidewalk of a busy street, looked up to see a maroon Dodge convertible (with the top down) full of laughing white kids speed off down the boulevard. In an instant he sprinted after them, running right down the middle of the street for all he was worth.

The foolish teens hadn't counted on this, nor did they anticipate the light turning red, and the car in front of them drawing to a halt, blocking their path of escape. A sense of panic filled the car, as the frantic kids looked back to see a very angry black guy bearing down on them.

Bobby ran up beside the car and dove right into the middle of it. He was like a man possessed, swinging at every one of them. The four kids couldn't get out of the car fast enough, running for their lives down the street and leaving Bobby in a fit of laughter in their abandoned vehicle.

While it was true that Bobby Lloyd would throw punches at the slightest provocation, it would be wrong to characterize him as a bully. The truth is that he gained no satisfaction from pushing around weaker people. In fact, one of his greatest sources of satisfaction in life was to be able to protect loved ones who looked up to him.

One such situation occurred in the summer of 1963 in the mostly white neighborhood adjoining his. It all began when a black kid named Peanut Baker got the better of another kid named

Andre Thompson in a fistfight. Well, Andre's older brother beat up Peanut and back and forth it went until a number of friends and family members from both sides were involved in the feud.

It just so happened that the Thompson family lived next door to Russell Jack and his family. Peanut Baker was a member of an informal gang of kids led by Stevie Lloyd and so it was inevitable that big brother Bobby would eventually become involved in the dispute.

****

It was a hot, humid summer evening. Word had reached the Thompsons that trouble was brewing. Mr. Thompson shared his concerns with Hugh Jack (Russell's father, Adele's husband) knowing he was a high school coach who was accustomed to breaking up fights. Don't misunderstand. Mr. Thompson was an enormous man who could hold his own. He didn't fear anyone, but he was also wise enough to want to avoid trouble whenever possible.

The two were standing in the Thompson front yard when they saw a dozen bat-wielding kids making their way down the street, led by a hatchet-toting Stevie Lloyd. They took one look at the anger on his face and knew they wouldn't be able to reason with him. The Thompson boys took their place behind the two adults as the menacing gang approached.

Mr. Jack was determined to assume the peacekeeper role that he had performed so many times before at the high school. He tried to reason with Stevie but, as anticipated, the teenager was having no part of it. He wanted blood.

Just then, when it looked as though the situation was about to break into a full-scale rumble, Bobby Lloyd pulled up in his '55 Chevy. He jumped out of the car and rushed between the two groups.

"Stevie, get outta here," he barked. The fierce countenance on his younger brother's face withered into compliance. He would never consider talking back to his older brother. Such was the enormous respect he held for him. Without another word spoken, the entire gang turned right around and marched back down the street from where they came.

No one knew how Bobby found out about the incident or how he knew when to show up. But this incident established a deep friendship with the Jack family that now extended beyond Russell.

In fact, it wasn't long before Bobby started becoming a fixture at their house. He was especially fascinated by Mrs. Jack and her deep convictions about the need for racial equality. He even accompanied her to Dr. Martin Luther King Jr.'s historic march on Washington D.C. that occurred a few months later.

Even more significant than his growing friendship with Russell and his parents, was the relationships that would eventually develop with three other family members. Dianne, no more than a skinny, freckle-faced adolescent at this time, was seven years his junior. Hughie was a year behind her and Jimmy, the baby of the family, five years behind Hughie.

It was these encounters with this white family that would earn him the title "The Black Knight," dubbed this by Mr. Jack because Bobby was black and always showed up after midnight. One example of Bobby's protective attitude toward them occurred a couple of years after the incident with the Thompsons.

Hughie was playing with a black kid named Oscar who was a little older than him. A tire was hanging from a limb in the tree in front of Oscar's home. The two kids were swinging it back and forth, when Oscar suddenly pushed it with all his might. The tire sailed straight into the younger kid's face, knocking Hughie down and leaving him with a black eye.

Hughie just chalked it up to roughhousing fun and began heading for home. Bobby happened by in his Chevy and noticed the kid's shiner standing out glaringly against his white skin.

He whipped his car to the curb and got out to check it out. In a look that would become "trademark Bobby Lloyd," he peered over his shades at the kid's bruised face. "Alright, what happened?" he questioned.

"Oh, Oscar and I were just tossin' a tire back and forth and I got hit in the eye."

"I'll take care of it," was Bobby's ominous answer, as he got back into his car.

Hughie didn't think anything of the brief conversation until a few days later when he ran into Oscar at school. The older boy had two black eyes and a broken nose. "What happened?" Hughie asked, with real concern.

"Nothin' happened." Oscar was clearly afraid to talk to him. Hughie found out later that Bobby had threatened Oscar's life if he ever hurt the white boy again. He felt bad for his friend, and yet, at the same time, greatly appreciated the sense of security he felt having Bobby Lloyd, "The Black Knight," as his protector.

****

Then there was the time a group of local junkies slipped into the Jack house in the middle of the night, looking for something to steal. The desperate thieves rummaged through the home, stepping right over kids sleeping on the living room floor. One of them discovered the brand new stereo Mr. Jack had just purchased and carted it out the front door.

Another one of the black guys boldly entered the parents' bedroom, searching for valuables. He noticed Adele's purse, sitting on the nightstand not more than a few inches from her face, but as he reached for it, the middle-aged-woman woke up and began screaming. The startled junkie ran out of the room and flew down the stairs. By now the whole house was in an uproar, as the intruders dashed off into the night.

Right away Mrs. Jack called Bobby Lloyd, who showed up within minutes along with a couple of his guys. By this time, Bobby had become the unofficial leader of a gang of toughs. All four of the young black men were wearing the matching black leather jackets and hats broken down in the stylish fashion of the day. Yeah, by this time the Rockville brothers had become more serious… more dangerous.

Immediately, Bobby took control of the situation, ordering each of his boys to check out different areas around the house. Pretty soon they had all returned, empty-handed. Whoever did the job had fled the scene.

"Alright," said Bobby, "I'll take care of it." That's all he said and within two days, he had returned all of the missing articles. As usual, there was no explanation.

One of Bobby's most pronounced characteristics was his penchant for privacy. His approach to crime and violence was precisely the opposite of those fools who can't wait for the opportunity to brag about their exploits. Bobby kept everything close to the vest, never talking about such situations. Those closest to him knew better than to ask.

Years passed before Bobby confided to anyone that he had paid a visit to the Bee Hive tavern later that day and put the word out that he wanted every single item returned by that night—or else. And that's exactly what happened. Even junkies, desperate for their next fix, knew better than to cross Bobby Lloyd. His reputation was already becoming powerful in the black communities on Long Island.

Loretta's daughters
Chante and little Bobbette
Sing Sing 1977

Bobby in 1971

CHAPTER EIGHT

The Powder Game

The whole country's going crazy! Bobby thought. It was true. By 1969, body bags by the hundreds were being shipped back to the States from an exotic country called Viet Nam; the "free love" movement birthed in Haight-Ashbury had given way to an underground culture built around drug abuse. The sexual revolution had begun to sweep the country, leaving in its wake what we see today: unwanted pregnancies, STDs, hardcore pornography, child abuse, and pedophilia. The peaceful civil rights movement—championed by Bobby Kennedy and Dr. Martin Luther King Jr.—had been cut down by assassins' bullets and replaced by a leftist group of radicals called the Black Panthers.

Bobby was detached from most of this chaos. He was working as a mechanic at a gas station in Lakeview, married to Cheryl, who gave birth to his second daughter, Monique. A slave to his insatiable sexual appetite, his side-kick Loretta conceived his third daughter, Chante Caprice. Concurrently, Cheryl was again pregnant with their second child, a fourth daughter, Dawn. (A few years later, Loretta would give him his fifth daughter, Bobbette.) Little did Bobby know how drastically his life was about to change through a couple of unconnected and seemingly insignificant events.

The first of these occurred one day at the gas station when a sleek, gray Cadillac pulled in. Bobby dutifully started filling the man's gas tank, while, at the same time, drinking in the picture that had just presented itself.

The driver was a sharply dressed black man in his thirties who had success written all over him. More noteworthy than the nice clothes or elegant ride were the two gorgeous black girls accompanying him. They both possessed that rare beauty that can easily take a girl to Hollywood. Bobby took all of this in as he topped off the man's gas tank and approached him for payment. The guy pulled a huge knot of money out of his front pants' pocket.

"You're Bobby Lloyd." It was simply a statement of fact.

"Yeah," he responded, wondering how a man like this could know about *him*.

"I've been told about you," the man said, mentioning a couple of mutual acquaintances and introducing himself as Supe. "Listen, why don't you take a ride with me? I need someone to watch my back."

It was an exciting prospect for the 24-year-old, but one he couldn't accept. "I'm working, man."

"Listen, I'll pay you twice as much as you'll make here," Supe assured him.

That's all he needed to hear. After telling his boss he was sick, Bobby met his new friend down the street and drove off with him.

All day long the four drove through Queens and Manhattan, repeating the same basic scene over and over. Supe would walk into a bar, Bobby a step behind him, literally "watching his back." He would retrieve a lunch bag—the contents of which he guessed to be money—and then they would get back into the car and drive to the next location.

At the end of the day, Supe brought him back to where Bobby had left his car and handed him three $100 bills. "I'll be in touch," was all he said as he drove off.

****

It wasn't but a couple of weeks later that the second significant incident happened. Bobby was at the Bee Hive when Meat, a long time friend, handed him a tiny spoon packed with white powder. "Try this, man."

"What is it?" Bobby asked, as he took a matchbook and folded the cover on an angle.

Meat brushed aside his concerns. "Just put it up to your nose and sniff it. You'll like it."

Bobby did so, but within moments, he became overwhelmed with nausea and had to run for the bathroom. *What's the point in this?* he wondered as he returned to the table. He quickly found out when he sat down and an overwhelming sense of tranquility overcame him. *Man, I've never felt so mellow*, he thought dreamily to himself. Bobby liked this new feeling. In fact, he liked it a lot. "What is this stuff?" he asked again.

"That's the big H, man!" replied Meat triumphantly. "You know, stuff, smack, junk."

A few nights later he ran into his friend again. "Hey Meat, let me have another snort of that smack," insisted Bobby.

"Hey man, that stuff costs money!" Meat protested. "I can't be supporting your high. You gotta pay for it, man."

And Bobby did so and continued to do so with increasing regularity.

In the meantime, Supe showed up again, offering Bobby a regular job. For the next year or so, a couple times a week, he would ride along with his mentor, picking up bags just like he did that first day.

At first, Bobby didn't realize he had entered the "powder game." Bobby also didn't put together that what Meat was doing, so was Supe. Over time Supe began teaching him the tricks of the trade of selling heroin. "You know you could be doing this yourself, Bobby," he finally told him.

"Oh, yeah?" Bobby was intrigued.

"Listen," said Supe, taking on a patronizing tone, as if he were explaining the facts of life to a youngster. "I'll sell you a load of stuff, which is 30 bags, for $15. You can turn around and sell those bags for a ten spot apiece."

"Wow! That's quite a profit!" Bobby was starting to get excited at the prospects.

And so it was that Bobby Lloyd became a heroin user and dealer almost simultaneously.

But Bobby Lloyd was destined for more success than the average dealer. Not only did he possess the fearlessness and common sense to do well in this business, but he also had two other important elements going for him.

First, he was getting a very pure form of heroin at a good price from Supe, and Jimmy, Supe's cousin. Most of the powder players were selling junk that had been stepped on with quinine powder as many as fifteen times. Bobby cut his too, but it didn't take long before word got out on the streets that he had the best smack available.

The second thing he had going for him—as was the case for all serious dealers—was a qualified tester: a junkie with a high tolerance to heroin. Gary, Bobby's tester, was extremely valuable to the operation because he could give him a good idea of the quality of the stuff, and if it happened to be pure, he could do it without overdosing. So when Bobby would go to purchase a quantity, he would take Gary along to test it. Not only did this protect him from paying top dollar for weak powder, but it also let him know how many times he should step on it before sending it out to the streets. Gary? He got a free high on what was usually very good stuff.

As word hit the streets that Bobby was selling powerful stuff, guys started coming to him from other communities on Long Island—both black and white. Now, instead of buying a load, he began copping quarter spoons or even a half an ounce at a time. Little by little, he was getting away from doing "hand-to-hand-combat" (dealing to users) and entering into the "weight business" (selling to small time dealers). Because of the quality of the heroin he was getting, Bobby quickly became very successful.

Success brought added danger, though. The high amount of traffic coming to him made him too visible for the small black neighborhood of Rockville Centre. So he rented an apartment in a high-crime section of Queens, where people had long since learned it was safer to mind one's own business. This new pad was only made available to a few select dealers.

Bobby knew he could no longer operate at this level without help, so he hired Kevin, Ricky, and Godfrey—guys he knew and trusted. They cut and packaged the heroin, acted as his bodyguards, occasionally picked up fresh supplies, and took turns manning the apartment and selling to other dealers.

Bobby Lloyd had just entered the big leagues. He was becoming a serious player in the dangerous world of powder.

The Black Caddy
1978

Blue Notes
1979

CHAPTER NINE

Caught in the Web

"Whoa, what happened to you?!" exclaimed Bobby, clearly impressed with the vision that had just presented itself.

"I guess I grew up," responded Dianne cheerfully. Russell Jack's little sister had undergone a dramatic metamorphosis since Bobby had last seen her. It was more than the fact that she was now a blond-haired, green-eyed 18-year-old worthy of notice. There was a wildness to her spirit that enhanced her natural beauty.

The occasion of this re-acquaintance was Russell's wedding reception. By the time Bobby showed up, Dianne had already been turning heads with her gold sequined mini-dress, black satin bell-bottoms, and spiked platform heels.

Little did he know that she had had a crush on him since the first time she saw him eight years earlier. The thought that Bobby Lloyd, the legend of Rockville Centre himself, would take notice of her was thrilling.

The two casually talked for awhile before Bobby invited her to go for a ride. Dianne opened the heavy door of the black Cadillac and slid onto the tan leather seat. For the next two hours she rode around with the "Black Knight," as her father had coined him. This wasn't merely a joyride. Bobby was taking care of business: first picking up a lunch bag stuffed with who-knows-what at a bar in Queens and then driving through the Midtown Tunnel into Manhattan where he met with a group of dangerous looking characters in front of a corner drug store. It was all so exciting to a teenager in love.

The truth is, Dianne didn't much care where they went—she was exhilarated that her long-held dream seemed to be coming true. Eventually they ended up in a hotel, where her fantasy reached its culmination. The next morning Bobby dropped her off at home. "I'll be in touch," he said as she left his car.

For three days Dianne beamed with joy and for three days she hovered over the telephone, waiting, listening, hoping. And then, true to his word, Bobby called, promising to pick her up at nine o'clock that night.

The hours crawled along as the elated girl prepared for The Event. Fanciful dreams of marriage, a house, and children filled her girlish imagination. The great procedure for such a night out began at six o'clock, when she couldn't take another tormenting moment of idleness.

The first order of business was the choice of the evening's outfit. She didn't want to appear too brazen, but she also wanted to make sure that the presentation captivated his attention. After laboring over her best dresses, she finally settled on a bright red blouse with a black mini-skirt and thigh high boots.

After showering, scenting her body, meticulously toiling over every eyelash, applying just the right amount of make-up—all of which was checked and rechecked—she finally pronounced herself ready.

She emerged from the bathroom, unnoticed by her unimpressed siblings apart from the choice words of irritation supplied by ten-year-old Jimmy, aggravated that he had been denied the bathroom for over two hours.

The princess descended the stairs to await the arrival of her prince. She plopped down on the couch and whiled away the next hour watching sitcoms with her dad. Nine o'clock finally arrived, but Bobby didn't arrive with it. *He'll be here*, she reassured herself. Sitcoms were now replaced with a detective story, which was followed by another and another. The expectant girl remained at her post until, around midnight when she finally dozed off on the couch.

"Dianne, Dianne," the voice penetrated her sleep, as a hand gently nudged her shoulder. "Dianne, you better go to bed. I don't think Bobby's coming tonight," said her father compassionately. The heartsick girl climbed the stairs to her lonely room where she cried herself back to sleep in private.

The next day an apologetic Bobby called promising to make it up to her. This time he showed up—although an hour late—and took her cruising to some of his favorite haunts. The wonderful evening erased the previous night's ordeal, and the romantic fantasy once again gained steam.

It wasn't to last.

The novelty of her fling with the "Black Knight" had worn itself out after suffering through several more painful, humiliating no-shows. His next phone call received a cool reception. "You know what? I can't do this anymore, Bobby."

****

Dianne was special to Bobby for a number of reasons. First and foremost, she was a member of the Jack family; that alone made her special. Of course, it didn't hurt that she was beautiful either. But the one thing that really intrigued him was her untamed spirit.

Although he hadn't seen her in a long time, Russell had shared with him some of her exploits—especially of her willingness to fight. During her younger years, Dianne had been involved in dozens of fights with other girls—and sometimes even with guys. One time she had even thrown a girl off a balcony, breaking her back.

Bobby hadn't been too concerned when he heard she was smoking pot and occasionally taking psychedelics. In the late '60s, this was becoming the norm.

After their short-lived fling, Bobby and Dianne became good, if only occasional, friends. She eventually acquired a "head shop" in Rockville Centre, and Bobby, always the big brother and family protector, started sending his boys over to buy stuff—whether they needed it or not.

Before long, his crew began cutting and packaging their dope at her shop. "Does Bobby pay you for this?" asked one of his guys one day.

"No, he doesn't give me money," she replied.

"Well, take this," he said, handing her a quart baggie full of heroin. "Just please don't tell him I gave it to you."

Dianne didn't want to seem ungrateful and so accepted the package, but as soon as they left, dumped it down the toilet, oblivious to the fact it was worth a thousand bucks on the street. This routine repeated itself a number of times in the coming months. She never said anything to Bobby, afraid he would kill the guy for giving her uncut heroin.

One day she absent-mindedly threw the baggie into a cookie jar and forgot about it. Not long after that she went on a binge of LSD and angel dust. In the past she had brought herself down with "Reds" (a street tranquilizer), but she didn't have any this time. Just then she recalled the times Bobby would nod out after snorting heroin and—as if some unseen force had planned the entire episode—she simultaneously remembered the bag of heroin in the cookie jar. She snorted a little and instantly felt a great calm come over her, soon replaced by much needed sleep.

To her surprise, she really enjoyed this strange, euphoric sensation and began returning to the cookie jar again and again. Eventually the inevitable addiction began to conquer her and she started going to the streets looking for more, because Bobby got busted and was in the "pen" (prison). Like most junkies, her habit of snorting heroin eventually gave way to main lining (injecting) once she realized how much more potent it was. Dianne was on a dangerous road into hell, as she found herself needing to purchase increasingly greater amounts to ward off the wretched sickness.

She soon discovered that Harlem offered the best heroin, so that's where Dianne would go. Her main connection was a black guy who did his trade from a burned out tenement on 114th Street near Lenox Avenue. The structure had once been a beautiful brownstone apartment building, but the ravages of inner city life had worn it down—first as an overcrowded tenement, and then finally, to its present condition, unfit for human habitation.

One sweltering day in August 1971, Dianne was particularly desperate to get high. The dreaded sickness had already brought on an episode of retching. Her eyes watered, her skin crawled, and her nerves were on end. She made the drive through Queens, across the Tri-Borough Bridge, and on into Harlem.

The frantic girl brought her old Chevy to a lurching halt near the structure, hoping to see her pusher in his usual spot out front. He wasn't there so she fearlessly barged into the shooting gallery in search of him. As her eyes adjusted to the dim surroundings, she noticed that the building was thick with junkies: some in the nod of bliss, others retching, one vomiting in a corner.

She eventually found her man arguing with another junkie about a subject she should have paid attention to, but she was too desperate to think clearly. The verbal battle halted as she approached. "I need a couple of bags, man," she told him with strained voice.

"Twenty bucks," came the abrupt reply. Dianne pulled two ten spots out of her pocket and exchanged it for the tiny bags, hurrying out of the building to her car.

She got into the passenger seat, retrieved her works out of the glove box, and began to prepare her fix. First she dumped the white contents of the tiny bag into a tablespoon, sporting a strangely bent handle that allowed it to sit perfectly level on a hard surface. After pouring the contents of one of the bags into the spoon, mixing it with water, and heating it to a quick boil, she drew up the liquid into her syringe.

She looped a belt around her left bicep, cinching it tight with her teeth and jabbing the needle into her vein. As the contents disappeared from the plastic tube and entered her blood stream, she awaited the end of that day's nightmare—only it didn't come. After a couple of minutes, it became painfully obvious she had been ripped off!

Dianne flew out of her car and confronted the man, who had positioned himself back in his usual spot outside of the building. "I want my money back and I want it back now!" she demanded. He was a big man, not accustomed to being challenged by men, let alone women. His eyes darted around the street, deciding how best to handle this new drama. By this point, Dianne had realized the reason the other junkie had been confronting him.

Dianne was furious, sick, and desperate. "If you don't give me my money back right now I swear I will slice your face open from ear to ear!" she screamed, as she reached into her purse.

"What's wrong?" he asked, feigning ignorance.

"You gave me milk sugar and you know it!"

"Man, they must have ripped me off. I swear I didn't know anything about it!" he lied.

Murder was clearly in her eyes. "Just give me my money!"

"Okay, okay," he acquiesced. Fortunately for Dianne, he thought $20 unworthy of so much trouble.

Thanks to Bobby Lloyd, Dianne Jack had become hooked on heroin. And thus, one of the very people Bobby had committed to protect had become a victim of the death in which he was trading.

with
Rusty (the gun)

CHAPTER TEN

Hustles on the Streets

As soon as Bobby saw George, he knew something was wrong. George was a Jewish insurance agent whom he had befriended years before. He was also a petty criminal, occasionally dabbling in shady business practices on the side.

"What's wrong, George?" inquired Bobby.

"Bobby, I need some help," answered an agitated George. "I have a client, a Jewish woman, who allowed her $50,000 life insurance policy on her husband to lapse. Well, the man died last month, and she called to ask me if there is anything I could do to get her policy reinstated. I told her I could probably do it, but it would cost her fifteen grand," he continued. "She agreed to pay me, so I told our home office that I had made a mistake and, sure enough, they reinstated her policy and paid her. But once she got her money, she refused to pay me."

"I'll get your money for you," offered Bobby. "Just give me her address." This was classic Bobby Lloyd: ready to do nearly anything for a friend, even when risk was involved.

That very day Bobby and Eddie paid her a visit. The lady answered the door of her stately residence. She eyed the two black men suspiciously through the cracked door. "What do you want?" she asked, a sense of superiority dripping from every one of her four words.

Bobby ignored her question and her attitude, sticking his right foot in the doorway so she couldn't close it. The smug widow's face blanched. "What are you doing?" she asked with alarm in her voice.

"You owe somebody some money," said Bobby with danger in his voice. "And you better pay him. If you don't, I'll be back and you're not going to like what I'm going to do." The two bullies casually walked back to their car and drove off.

The greedy woman called George three hours later. "Meet me at the bank," she said tersely. "I'll give you your money; just don't ever send your friends around here again." George received his dues that afternoon, his admiration for Bobby growing considerably.

****

It wasn't but a month later when another white friend came to Bobby for help. Tony was a big Italian who could handle himself, yet he was clearly frightened about something.

"Bobby, I owe some people money," said Tony. "But I know how we can come up with it."

"What do you mean *we*?" asked Bobby, guessing that "some people" meant members of the Mafia.

"I know I can count on you, Bobby," continued the distraught man. "Listen, I know a guy who just got ten jars of reds. He'll be easy pickin's for us. Bobby, I gotta pay those dudes off."

Bobby considered the situation momentarily, weighing the dangers involved against his friendship with Tony. *Those people don't know me*, he reasoned, assuring himself that he wouldn't have to face retribution later. "Alright, Tony, I'll help you out."

The two retrieved their pistols and drove to Queens, parking in front of an apartment building whose best days were in the past. The salt-and-pepper team approached the second-floor apartment cautiously. Tony gave three rapid raps on the door. "Who is it?" came the reply from inside.

"It's Tony."

As soon as the door opened, both men brandished their weapons, Tony putting his revolver in the face of the man who answered the door. Bobby remained at the door, aiming his .38 at the three guys sitting on a tattered gold couch. "Get over against the wall and don't say a word," yelled the Italian.

"Tony, whaddya doin'?" asked his bewildered friend.

"I'm sorry man, but I need those reds." Just then a girl came out of a bathroom down the hall. Bobby whirled around, ready to shoot, prompting a fit of screaming from her. "Shut up!" barked Bobby.

"Where are they?" Tony demanded.

"In the closet on the floor, Tony." The man seemed more concerned about being betrayed than about the loss of the barbiturates. In four giant steps the Italian was at the closet. He pulled the grocery bag out of the cubicle, quickly rummaged through it with his hand, and walked straight out the door. Bobby backed out behind him.

The next day Bobby saw a very relieved Tony. "They're paid," he said triumphantly. "I owe you, Bobby."

You better believe it.

****

"Lee, you strappin'?" Bobby asked. It was 11 o'clock on a Saturday night.

"My piece is in the house," answered his cousin.

"Go get it," said Bobby grimly. "We gotta take care o' some business."

The two men slid into Bobby's Caddy and proceeded to pick up Kevin and Ricky—and their guns. By this time, Bobby and the "soldiers" he had gathered around him were a fearsome team. Lee was his 18-year-old cousin. Kevin and Ricky had both established violent reputations.

Bobby was silent on the quick jaunt to Hempstead, only telling them he was looking for Gerard Watts. "He still ain't paid me that money," he snapped.

The jive talk that typically erupted when the four were togeth-er was conspicuously absent. The mood became even more somber when Bobby pulled up in front of The Shanty. It was known as a dangerous bar—not the kind of place you just dropped in for a drink—but it was also the most likely place to find Gerard.

The bar was in full swing by the time they got there. The parking lot was packed with an assortment of Cadillacs, Lincolns, and even a couple of Mercedes. "He's here," Bobby announced to his crew. "There's his ratty New Yorker," he said with disdain.

It would be a stretch to call it a nightclub, although its owner did his utmost to make it appear as one. There were nearly fifty people crowded around card tables or along the L-shaped bar, talking excitedly, laughing, and carrying on. Two couples were shuffling, twirling, and grinding on the tiny dance floor—their sensuous, athletic endeavors more an exhibition for the hooting audience than for personal enjoyment.

Suddenly, Bobby burst through the door, Lee on his heels. Kevin and Ricky followed them in, taking their stand—hands inside their coats—on either side of the front door. Lee took his place ten feet behind his elder cousin, observing everything and everyone. No one would be leaving this establishment until Bobby's business was resolved.

The music in the jukebox continued blaring, but everything—everything—else came to an utter standstill. Bobby Lloyd had murder on his face. His reputation for controlled ferocity was well known. He wasn't mean for mean's sake, but when he meant business he was dangerous.

As Bobby scanned the party looking for Gerard, he didn't encounter the defiant, hostile glares one would expect from such a crowd, but the unmistakable look of fear. Every eye in the house was fixed on him—waiting to see what he would do.

Bobby's contracting eyebrows and narrowing eyes exhibited the intensity of boiling wrath. *There he is*, he announced to himself, moving swiftly through the accommodating crowd.

"Yo, Gerard. Where's my money?" It wasn't a simple question but a life-or-death demand.

Maybe Gerard's girlfriend felt safe amongst her friends. Whatever the case, she decided to take up his cause. "Who you think..."

Bobby slapped her so hard she flew into a table and landed in a heap. Gerard looked terrified and Bobby slapped him too, just for good measure. "I'm going to ask you one more time," he said deliberately. "Where's my money?"

"Uh, well, uh, I have some here," Gerard stammered, pulling a wad of bills out of his front pocket. Bobby glanced at it, figuring it to be no more than a hundred bucks or so.

"The next time I see you, you better have my money," Bobby snarled. "If I don't see you tomorrow, I'll have a good surprise for ya." With that, he strode out, his men covering him as they backed out of the bar.

It was actually four days later before Gerard showed up with the money. "Man, Bobby, I was gonna pay you," he whined. "You didn't have to shame me in front of all my friends."

"Listen," snipped Bobby. "I've killed people for less than that."

Incidents like these continued to build Bobby Lloyd's reputation—one that was becoming known in ever greater crime circles throughout New York City.

Bobby hated people like Gerard. One of his partners in crime named Bootsy had someone who took his money and never gave Bootsy the goods. So Bobby, Meat, and Bootsy went to Brooklyn several times that month in search of the guy. The waste of time had Bobby so mad, he could have removed the guy. Long story short: he paid.

Bobby on Easter

George and Jeff Lane

CHAPTER ELEVEN

The Black Mob

Bobby's expanding realm of influence was about to bring him into a whole new level of crime. The New York heroin industry of the '70s was controlled by the Mafia. Two of the major players at the time were brothers Frank and Matty Madonna, members of the Lucchese Mafia family.

Their involvement began in the early '60s when they developed strong overseas connections. They imported heroin and stockpiled a virtual mountain of it in various tenement buildings scattered throughout the small Italian district of East Harlem. Most New York junkies were African-Americans and the challenge for the two Italian brothers was to find a way to move that white gold into the veins of those ebony-colored arms.

While serving time in prison, Matty Madonna met a smalltime hood named Leroy "Nicky" Barnes. Matty recognized leadership qualities in Barnes that he felt could be utilized to build a black drug empire—one which he could supply.

"If you wanna be protected from the powder," Matty instructed his protégé, "you gotta treat it like you're the don. You want all the profit to flow up, and all the risks to flow down." He went on to describe an organization complete with captains and soldiers. "You need at least three levels between you and the powder," he went on, "'cause each level is a layer of protection." [2]

An unlikely relationship developed between the two, and when Nicky was released, he immediately set about building

2 Leroy 'Nicky' Barnes and Tom Folsom, *The Rise and Fall of the Black Godfather: Mr. Untouchable,* Milo Books Limited, New York, 2007, p. 31.

his organization. His first move was to gather around himself six other experienced gangsters whom he trusted, forming a leadership team they coined "The Council." Then, just as Matty had shown him, they each hired captains (wholesale dealers) and soldiers (mid-level dealers) who, in turn, "pushed" the drugs out to those doing hand-to-hand-combat on the streets.

The Council now began receiving large quantities of heroin from the Italians, moving it down the chain of command where it could reach the teeming masses of shivering, retching junkies populating the streets of New York City. By the early '70s, The Council was moving a hundred kilos of powder per month, realizing an annual income of $72 million—an enormous amount of money in the economy of that day.

"Nicky Barnes," conceded the New York Times, "had made a fortune flooding black neighborhoods with heroin" and was swaggering around as "an invincible outlaw."[3]

"Prosecutors saw Barnes as a public menace to put in prison—and found it maddeningly difficult to get him headed there. Nicky Barnes had been arrested for homicide, bribery, drug dealing, and possession of dangerous weapons. But none of the charges stuck. Impressed by his apparent ability to beat any rap, blacks called him 'Mr. Untouchable.'"[4]

In a business where nearly every customer, every competitor, and even one's employees, are viewing life through a criminal mindset—always, *always* looking for the opportunity to score something for nothing—discipline is the key to success. And Nicky Barnes was devoted to success. "You have to use violence as a means to resolve certain problems," Barnes said later, justifying his ruthlessness. "That's the way this game is played and it's

---

3 Sam Roberts, "Crime's 'Mr. Untouchable' Emerges From Shadows" *New York Times*, March 4, 2007.

4 Fred Ferretti, "Bad, Bad Leroy Barnes" *New York Times Magazine*, December 12, 1977.

always been played this way. And if you don't see it, you won't survive. Anybody who's in power who's not willing to [murder] will be terminated."[5]

"It isn't personal," adds Leon 'Scrap' Batts, one of his lieutenants. "It's just business. I like you and all, but you [messed] up and you gotta get this. It ain't what you owe, it's how you owe. You owe a guy money and then you disappear on him and then next week you're driving a brand new car—that's the ultimate insult, saying we soft. If you let one guy get away with that then everybody's going to get away with that, and then you have no strength and no power."[6]

Under Barnes' leadership, The Council thrived for almost a decade, reaching its pinnacle of success during the mid-70s. In the meantime, the helpless New York Police Department watched as one bloodied corpse after another appeared on the streets of Harlem. "We all had hot tempers and private graveyards," admitted Barnes later. "...if you're not willing to use violence in the drug game, you're not gonna survive. It's street-corner Darwinism."[7]

****

Bobby's induction into this crime family began in a most unlikely manner: tuna fish sandwiches prepared in a Queens' drugstore.

By now, George, the Jewish man Bobby had assisted, had forsaken his insurance career and had purchased an old-fashioned drugstore in Queens, complete with luncheon counter. George's

5 Leroy Barnes, quoted in the Damon Dash production, *Mr. Untouchable: Godfather or Snitch*; Magnolia Pictures/HDNet Films, in association with Dash Films and Blowback Productions (HDNet Films LLC, 2007).
6 Leon Batts, quoted in *Mr. Untouchable: Godfather or Snitch*.
7 Leroy 'Nicky' Barnes and Tom Folsom, *The Rise and Fall of the Black Godfather: Mr. Untouchable*, Milo Books Limited, New York, 2007, p. 128.

tuna fish sandwiches had gradually developed quite a following in the neighborhood.

One group, in particular, frequented his luncheon counter for those tuna sandwiches. George had no idea that the pack of likeable thugs worked for Solomon Glover, a lieutenant in the Barnes crime family. He also didn't realize this man was considered by Nicky Barnes himself to be "just a really dangerous dude." [8] The compact, stocky, dark-skinned brother was not only a hit man but was also responsible for supplying arms to the entire organization.

Bobby had heard plenty about Nicky Barnes on the streets, but he, too, had no idea that the gang hanging out across the street from George's drugstore was one of his crews. But over time, as he occasionally visited George, he got to know Earnest, one of Solomon's men. As their friendship grew, they realized how much they shared in common. Each was a mid-level pusher with a number of street dealers under his charge.

It seemed inevitable that Bobby would meet Solomon Glover himself, and Earnest provided the introduction one night when he suggested that Bobby ride with him over the bridge into Harlem to get some product. The two dealers got into Earnest's customized Thunderbird and made the quick jaunt over the bridge, heading for Nicky Barnes' after-hours club. As was so often the case, Solomon was late for the appointment, so the two went to a local bar on 7th Avenue to wait for him. After about an hour, they cruised back by the club on 117th Street. "He's here," Earnest said, spotting Solomon's Eldorado. "Come on in with me."

Earnest and Bobby entered the dark room. "Hey, Solly," Earnest said cheerfully.

---

8 Leroy 'Nicky' Barnes and Tom Folsom, *The Rise and Fall of the Black Godfather: Mr. Untouchable,* Milo Books Limited, New York, 2007, p. 159.

The man eyed Bobby suspiciously. "Who's he?" the mobster asked grimly. "You know I don't do business around strangers."

"He's cool, man. We've been hangin' for the last few months," Earnest assured him. "He's a friend of George's."

"Yo, man. You know what? I'll wait outside," Bobby interjected. "You ain't got no problem with me, brother."

A moment of silent evaluation passed. "Hey, if you're alright with George, you're alright with me," came Solomon's verdict.

Following their initial encounter, Bobby began running into Solomon Glover at the drugstore and at various joints in Harlem and Queens. They would discuss insignificant things, most often their cars and their women. After several months passed, Solomon suggested he try out his product one day. "It's top quality." From then on, Bobby started getting his drugs from Glover.

Bobby's reputation as a standup guy was being increasingly established around Harlem. But he could tell that Solly was still a little unsure of him. One day he called Bobby. "Listen, Bobby, I need your help with something. Meet me at the Seville Lounge at two o'clock this afternoon."

"Sure, Solly. I'll be there."

Bobby struggled with conflicting emotions as he made the drive into Harlem that day. He was excited about the prospects that lay before him: getting in tight with Solomon, making even more money, building his reputation, and all the many benefits that were certain to follow such a move. But such possibilities did not come without grave concerns. For one thing, he knew that the closer he became affiliated with big names such as Solomon Glover and Nicky Barnes, the more the DEA* would become aware of him. He also had heard the rumors on the streets about

* The Drug Enforcement Agency is a department of the federal government that teams up with local police departments to investigate drug dealers.

the numerous murders surrounding the Barnes organization. *This is the big time*, Bobby told himself.

He pulled his Eldorado in front of the bar and waited. One hour, then two hours passed; no Solomon. By this time Bobby was impatiently standing alongside his car. Finally, a blue and white Eldorado pulled in behind his car. It wasn't Solomon's Cadillac so Bobby only glanced casually. But out of this car stepped a man so enormous that the car visibly lifted off the ground as he got out. He only stood about 6 feet 4 inches but must have weighed nearly 400 pounds. He was the most intimidating man Bobby had ever laid eyes upon.

"What's up, youngblood?" asked the giant. It was Smitty, Nicky Barnes' bodyguard. His words were friendly, but there was an unmistakable aura of evil about him.

"Nothing. I'm waitin' for a dude and he ain't here yet," responded Bobby.

"Who you waitin' for?"

No answer. Bobby knew better than to toss names around on the street.

"Let me guess," Goliath offered. "Is he a short, stocky dude who drives an Eldorado with a white top?"

"Yeah, that's my man."

"Well, you mize well chill, brother," chuckled the big man. "As long as I'm knowin' him, I ain't never known him to be on time for nuttin'."

"Man, I can't just be sittin' around here waitin' for him."

"Listen, if he told you to meet him here, you best wait for him. Believe me. He'll make it worth your while. What's your name, youngblood?"

"Bobby Lloyd."

"My name's Smitty," said he, offering his huge hand in a street handshake. "I've heard you're a standup guy, not afraid to mix it up."

"I do what I have to do," responded Bobby, a little sheepishly. He knew he was a good fighter, but what does that mean in the face of a beast like this?

"You gotta good rep. Just make sure you keep it that way." With that, Smitty proceeded into the bar.

Bobby considered what had just happened. He had heard plenty about Big Smitty on the streets. He was Nicky Barnes' personal bodyguard and had done time for killing a man with a machine gun. One could only guess how many men had met an early demise at his hands.

Man, how deep am I getting into this? Bobby thought. *Solomon wants me to do some job for him. Who knows what that's all about. Now I'm hooking up with men like Smitty, who would crush a man to death without a thought.* As usual, Bobby's ambitions quieted most of his fears.

An hour later, Solomon finally showed up, laughing as he got out of his Cadillac. He approached an un-amused Bobby. "Man, I been waitin' for three-and-a-half hours and you show up laughing!" he complained.

"That's the way it is, man. Deal with it," responded Solomon coolly. "Listen, I want you to help a friend of mine. I know I can trust you to do this job for me."

Bobby listened to him intently. He knew Glover was playing on his ego, but he didn't dare refuse him. As it turned out, he wanted Bobby to help him test the trustworthiness of another dude. Bobby took the project on, reporting his findings to Solomon the following week. "That's good, Bobby. I wanted to see how you would handle yourself. I've talked to the people who count. You're in."

He didn't need to elaborate. Bobby understood the implications. Like it or not, he was now part of the Nicky Barnes crime family.

Bobby's brother, Stevie with his wife, Diane
1971

CHAPTER TWELVE

Hounded, Hunted, and Held

Bobby was maneuvering his new black convertible Caddy (with a diamond in the back) across the grocery store parking lot when three unmarked police cars suddenly surrounded him. *Man,* he complained to himself, *what's this all about?* He brought his elegant ride to a stop and rolled down the window.

"Get out of the car," barked the middle-aged cop, approaching cautiously with gun drawn.

As Bobby complied, the DEA agent grabbed his right hand, wrenching it around his back and slamming him face first over the sprawling hood of the car. "I hate scum like you," he growled, jamming the barrel of his revolver into Bobby's right temple. Searing pain shot through his head, immediately demanding a physical response. Bobby was about to wheel around and kick the offending cop when one of the other agents arrived. "Come on Tom, this punk ain't worth it," he said calmly, pulling his wrathful partner away.

The six DEA agents meticulously searched the Cadillac, leaving its contents strewn across the parking lot. "He's clean," came the disappointing conclusion.

"Alright, Lloyd," said the more civil police officer. "You're free to go. But I want to tell you something," he said ominously. "It's only a matter of time."

Those words would ring over and over in Bobby Lloyd's mind in the days ahead.

CHAPTER 12

****

One day Bobby and Ricky drove to Harlem to pick up some product, which had already been packaged in quarter bags. A brown grocery bag held the treasure, which Bobby set down next to him on the floorboard of his Caddie as he prepared to make the jaunt back to Long Island. The pair cruised down 125th Street and, as they veered onto the Tri-Borough Bridge onramp, the bag fell over, scattering hundreds of white packets across the floor.

Bobby found himself in a serious dilemma for he was quickly approaching the toll booth. The duty officers who manned these booths had been trained by police to report suspicious activity. His first reaction was to look in his mirror for any police cars in the area and discovered, to his horror, that one was right behind him! He couldn't pull over on the bridge and Ricky was manning his customary bodyguard spot in the backseat.

"Ricky, get up here and gather this stuff up!" he yelled. It was a risky move, but there simply was no other option. Ricky climbed over the front seat and quickly shoveled all of the packets under the seat. Just as Bobby pulled alongside the booth, he looked down and noticed that Ricky had missed one packet, now sitting in plain view.

Don't panic! Bobby told himself. *Whatever you do, don't panic!* He handed two quarters to the attendant in the booth, who peered intently into the car as the coins dropped into his outstretched palm, then drove away as nonchalantly as he knew how. *He saw it! He looked right at it!* Bobby was in full-blown panic now.

No! he reasoned with himself. *It probably just looked like a scrap of white paper.* He was momentarily distracted from his schizophrenic inner argument as he looked in his mirror at the cop now approaching the booth.

"The cop's not comin' after us!" he told Ricky. "I bet he's callin' some of his partners ahead!" Sweat began pouring down his face. "Ricky, whaddya think?"

"I dunno, Bobby."

As the Cadillac approached the end of the bridge, Bobby turned down Northern Boulevard and began maneuvering through the side streets of Queens, rather than continuing on to Long Island. No police ever arrived. The entire drama was the typical paranoid mindset of a professional criminal. Rightly did Israel's King Solomon say, "The wicked flee when no one is pursuing..."

****

One day Bobby was visiting his brother Stevie when suddenly there was a sharp rap on the front door. "Who's there?" Stevie questioned, without opening the door.

"It's the police. Open the door."

Bobby sprang to his feet, ran upstairs and hid in the bathroom.

Stevie cracked the door. "Whaddya want?" he questioned.

"We have a warrant for your brother's arrest. Let us in," he demanded.

"My brother ain't here," he said, opening the door a little more.

"We know he's here," the cop yelled, pushing right past him. "His car's out front."

"He left his car here yesterday," Stevie protested. "I don't know where he's at now."

By now Stevie's quick-thinking wife had joined Bobby in the bathroom, turning on the shower. Cops fanned out through the house, looking under beds, in closets and even in the kitchen cabinets.

Two officers ran upstairs, Stevie on their heels. "Who's in this bathroom?" a heavyset cop demanded.

"My wife's taking a shower and you ain't goin' in there!" said Stevie indignantly.

"We're not leaving until we've seen inside this bathroom."

Just then Dolores cracked the door. "What's the problem, officer?" she asked innocently, peeking around the door.

"Sorry Mrs. Lloyd. We just need to make sure your brother-in-law isn't in there," he said.

"He's not in here, officer," she answered, opening the door enough for him to peer inside and see that she was clad in a towel. Bobby held is breath, just out of his sight, behind the shower curtain.

"He's not anywhere in this house," added one of the other agents who had now arrived upstairs.

"Let's go," grumbled the lead detective.

As the DEA agents left, a relieved Bobby emerged from the bathroom, heading straight for a second-floor window. "Just what I was afraid of," he announced, scanning the neighborhood. "There's two cops in a car down the street where they can watch my car *and* the house."

How am I gonna get out of here? Bobby wondered, sitting back down on the couch. After a few minutes of pondering his new dilemma, he arrived at the solution. In a moment, he was on the phone with his trusted associate. "Ricky, I'm in a jam. I need you to pick Helen up and come over to my brother's house on Lichen Street," he said. "Bring Willie with you, too. And listen, there's some cops staking out the house down the street. Make sure they see you guys come in."

The three arrived within the hour. "Come on in the bathroom," he told Helen, one of his girlfriends. "I need your clothes." Helen was taken aback by the statement but obediently followed him into the bathroom. A few minutes later the two came out, Helen in a bathrobe and Bobby dressed in her clothes.

The sight of Bobby Lloyd in drag was enough to send everyone to the floor in belly laughs. Bobby wasn't amused. "Man, you guys gotta take this serious," he earnestly told his thoroughly entertained friends.

A few minutes later, the two giggling hoods emerged from the house with their boss slinking along between them. The strange trio casually walked to Ricky's car, making good Bobby's getaway.

****

"Bobby, you have to turn yourself in," his lawyer told him over the phone. "They're looking all over for you."

"Okay, okay." That afternoon Bobby arrived at the police station. "I understand ya'll are lookin' for me."

Before the day was over, his attorney had him released on bail and the two were huddled over his desk examining the arresting officer's statement. The cop was alleging that Bobby had sold heroin to an undercover officer on April 14, 1973. "There ain't no way!" Bobby exclaimed, after reading that. "I was in Florida in April and I can prove it. We're fightin' this case," he said resolutely.

Two weeks later he arrived at court, ready to plead innocent to the charges. As he sat on the bench outside the courtroom awaiting his appearance before the judge, two detectives sat down, one on either side of him. "Just keep staring ahead and don't look at us," the cop to his right told him. "Listen, here's the deal. If you go in there and fight this case, we'll make sure you get fifteen years. We will lie through our teeth to put you away. Besides, who's going to believe a nigger over two police officers?" he continued. "We need a conviction on this case. Just plead guilty. The judge will give you six months and you'll be back on the streets in four."

Bobby knew there was no use in trying to fight these guys. It wasn't just the streets of New York City that were corrupt. He obediently entered his guilty plea and, just like they promised, received a six-month sentence. He did his four-month stint in Nassau County Jail and was soon back on the streets pushing his product.

First jail time
1973

Bobby, dressed to kill

CHAPTER THIRTEEN

Street Life

"Bobby, Bobby, I need to talk to you," said Ralph frantically.

"What's up, man?" responded an unruffled Bobby.

"There's a hit out on Stevie." Ralph was an excitable guy, so Bobby wasn't quick to buy into the story.

"What are you talkin' about, Ralph?"

"The word is that Chicago's got a hit on him," asserted Ralph.

"Naw, come on."

"Bobby, I'm tellin ya, there's a hit on him."

Why would Chicago have a beef with Stevie? Bobby wondered, as he got in his car and drove away. Even though Chicago was the sort of gangster who wouldn't hesitate to kill if necessary, the whole thing seemed too farfetched to be concerned about. After all, Stevie was a college graduate, well on his way to establishing a legitimate career as a bureaucrat.

A week later, Bobby heard the same story from a second source, this time with the reason: Stevie had been seeing the man's wife. Chicago had put the word out that he would pay $5,000 to anyone who would kill his wife's lover.

Bobby immediately confronted his brother. "Stevie, have you been messing around with Chicago's wife?"

"Yeah, I have," he admitted.

"Are you crazy? That man will kill you!"

"Bobby, this is what happened. I got to talking to this girl and it came out that we both love museums. So we went to a few museums together. She told me she was married but that her husband was doing five years in prison. He was outta the picture," he continued. "So, one thing led to another and before you know it, we're in the sack. Man, how was I supposed to know the guy would get an early release?"

"Stevie, I don't care what you have to do; you break it off with this girl! I'll take care of Chicago."

In spite of the fact that it was true, Bobby was surprised that Chicago would put a contract out on his brother. *He has to know this will start a war*, Bobby told himself, trying to make sense of it all. *I cannot believe he would be so brazen as to say he wants my brother killed.*

Bobby knew he had to confront the situation right away. He got Ricky and Willie and went straight to Chicago's house. He knocked on the door and Chicago answered it. Bobby grabbed him by the collar and jammed his .38 into his face. "Bobby, what's wrong? Bobby, what did I do? What's up?" he stammered, automatically raising his hands in submission.

"What are you doing putting a contract out on my brother? Are you out of your mind?"

"I ain't put no contract out on your brother!" Chicago insisted.

"Yes, you did."

"Bobby, the only guy I put a contract out on is a guy named Stevie who's been foolin' wit my wife."

"Chicago, that's my brother."

"But Bobby, he's been seeing my wife."

"Chicago, listen to me. I know you're not stupid," said Bobby, releasing his grip on the man and pulling his gun away. "If you hit my brother you know what's gonna happen."

"Bobby, if I would have known he was your brother, I would have came and talked to you. There wouldn't have been a contract."

"Alright, listen, I'll deal with my brother. He won't come around your wife again. But if anything happens to him, I'm comin' after you."

"You got it, Bobby. Man! You about scared me to death!"

****

By the early '70s, the African-American community was beginning to emerge from a long history of repression. This newfound success became especially evident in the field of entertainment. For a decade, Motown Records had been dazzling the music industry, serving up stars like Diana Ross, Stevie Wonder, and The Temptations. Hollywood moguls sought to capitalize on the situation as well and began producing "blaxploitation" films, such as *Shaft*.

Two of the productions at that time perfectly portrayed the life of Bobby Lloyd—now living large around New York City.

The first was William Devaughn's song, *Be Thankful For What You've Got*, which swept into top-forty music charts across the country. Its chorus became the mantra for the black criminal subculture and perfectly described Bobby's pride-and-joy:

Though you may not drive a great big Cadillac
Diamond in the back, sunroof top, diggin' the scene
With a gangsta lean
Gangsta whitewalls, TV antennas in the back

Even more descriptive of his life was the movie *Superfly*, [10] which followed on the heels of *Shaft*. The storyline revolves around Priest (played by Ron O'Neal), a Harlem cocaine dealer who longs

---

10 The author does not recommend this movie, if for no other reason than its sexually graphic scenes.

to escape the drug trade. He and his fast-talking partner Eddie have amassed $300,000 cash, which he wants to use to purchase 30 kilos of coke. He figures they can triple their money within a month and he can retire. The action-driven film is enhanced by the music of Curtis Mayfield. With songs like *Freddie's Dead* and *Pusherman,* the soundtrack actually generated greater profits than the film itself.

Everything about Priest's life—his interaction with dangerous acquaintances; his beautiful girlfriends—both black and white; his customized Eldorado complete with Rolls Royce hood ornament, heavily chromed front end and circular porthole windows; his tapered wardrobe, with bell-bottomed pants flaring out over black platform shoes, topped off with a Bosselino hat broken down to the side—all of it emblemized the black ghetto's conception of success. And all of it flawlessly depicted the life of Bobby Lloyd.

So when he heard the movie would be premiering in Manhattan, he knew he had to attend. Bobby picked up Ricky and Kevin and the trio arrived at the theater on opening night. The movie was all they hoped it to be. As the credits finished and the glaring lights were turned on, the three men started making their way down the steps from the balcony. It was then Bobby spotted Ron O'Neal, the movie's star, with two beautiful women walking parallel with them on the lower level. One of the girls looked up at Bobby and said, "Oh, honey, they're dressed just like you!" The chagrinned actor reproved the girl, undoubtedly informing her that the three men were the true-to-life essence of the movie. The crowd spilled out into the parking lot, Bobby's eyes catching Ron's as the two men approached their respective Cadillacs. The charismatic actor exchanged friendly glances with the gangster, offering a sheepish grin and a shrug of his shoulders: a fitting salute to a man who had built a successful career in crime.

Looking like Superfly
1971

Washington DC

CHAPTER FOURTEEN

𝕿𝖍𝖊 𝕭𝖎𝖌 𝕾𝖈𝖔𝖗𝖊

One day in early 1974, George asked Bobby to pay him a visit at the drugstore to discuss "a great idea."

"Bobby, let me ask you something," said George, leaning over his luncheon counter so only the intended could hear him. "What's the hottest drug on the street now?"

"Heroin," was the quick reply.

"Well, what's next?"

"That's easy: Daladid."

"What if we could get our hands on a bunch of it? Could you get rid of it?"

"Absolutely."

"I've got an idea, but I'll need your help with it," continued George.

"I'm listening."

"I found a drugstore for sale in New Jersey owned by two Chinese men. They want $100,000 for the store. I think we should buy it," he said confidently.

"Are you crazy? I ain't payin' a hundred grand for a drugstore! Besides, you already have one. Why would you want another one?"

"I'll explain it on the way over there. Let's go." Once Bobby grasped the plan, a huge grin stretched across his face. "Wow! What a great idea!"

Two hours later, they were in the store talking to the owners. There was at least twenty years difference in the two men. Wong, slightly hunched with a full rug of fine, white hair, must have been pushing seventy. His junior partner Kang was nearer forty and was clearly the more excitable of the two. He was also the only one who spoke English.

Bobby assumed the role of spokesman. "So, how much do you guys want for your store?"

"We want one hun-dwed thousand dolla," the younger man replied, sticking his chin out in a defiant gesture. "That include ev-wee-thing in building: fixt-ya, all the pwa-duck, dwug, skwipt pad; ev-wee-thing."

"That's a pretty steep price considering the neighborhood it's in," countered Bobby. It was important that he not seem too anxious. "I'll tell you what we'll do," continued Bobby. "We'll pay you $90,000 for it, $25,000 cash as a down payment. We'll take over the store right away and, within a month, we'll pay you the balance. But we need everything you got so we can make some of the money we need by the end of the month."

His offer elicited an eruption of Mandarin as the foreigners discussed the price. Wong seemed cautious, even reluctant, but Kang's reassurances seemed to win him over. "Okay, that a-gwee-able," the younger man finally said in his best deliberate English. "We wite up puchase a-gwee-ment."

"You're a man of your word aren't you?" responded Bobby.

"Of cowse," replied the Asian with mock indignation.

"Just write up a receipt for the $25,000. That's all we need."

Kang attempted to stifle the smile forcing itself across his face. "Okay, it a de-ow."

Bobby handed him an envelope of cash, which Wong promptly seized from Kang's hand, meticulously counting every bill. The two New Yorkers feigned great interest in every aspect of the operation as Kang showed them around the store. In reality, the buyers were only concerned about one item: the script pads used for ordering quantities of drugs. An hour later, the two Asians handed them the keys and walked triumphantly out the back door, leaving the store in the care of the new owners.

The partners wasted no time setting their plan into motion. They began ordering ten bottles of one hundred Daladids apiece every day. Jacob knew from his own experience that all narcotic orders are examined at the end of every month by an FDA auditor. Since he had planned his scheme to begin on the first day of the month, he knew they had nearly thirty days to order drugs. In the meantime, single orders of 1,000 pills were not enough to raise suspicions.

The shipments began arriving within forty-eight hours. Every day the Fed-Ex man would deliver the identical package containing 1,000 pills. Every day George or Bobby would dutifully sign his pad with a false name. Four weeks later, the two con men walked out of the store with over 25,000 pills to show for their efforts.

Before they left for good, Bobby approached a couple of adolescent black boys playing nearby. "Yo, what's up guys?"

"Ain't nothin'," replied the smaller one, trying to act tough.

"Guys, got any idea where the owner is to that drugstore?"

"No. Chinese dudes run that place."

"Well, the door's sittin' open and ain't no one in there," Bobby said, walking away.

He and George got in the Cadillac and circled the block, parking down the street where they could watch the show. Just as Bobby had expected, people were soon rummaging through the store, carrying out everything not bolted down. Within the hour, it was stripped clean. "Listen, if we happened to leave any trace of our identities in that place," Bobby explained to his Jewish partner, "I guarantee you, it's gone now."

They still had the challenge of selling the pills. Bobby didn't want to disrupt his normal flow of heroin by introducing an alternative to his clientele. He figured Solomon would be the best person from whom to seek advice. "Washington, man, that's where you'll get the highest price for Daladids," was his answer.

"That's where I'll go then," responded Bobby. *And I know just who to contact*, he thought to himself, Keggie

He arranged a meeting with an old friend, the girl he knew as Debbie in eighth grade, and drove down there the following day. "Keggie, how's it goin'?" Bobby asked her, as she slipped into his Eldorado.

"Things are good," she replied. "Man, you look good, Bobby. I ain't seen you in a long time."

"Yeah. Listen, I want you to try this out," he said, handing her one pill.

"Is this a Daladid?" she asked. "This is ten milligrams. Man, they're hard to come by."

"Yeah, all I've ever seen on the streets are fives," Bobby added.

Keggie swallowed the pill, rather than going through the hassle of getting all the necessary paraphernalia to shoot it up. Within a half hour her head was swimming. "Bobby, this is powerful!"

"Yeah. You think you could sell some if I got them to you?"

"You better believe it," she replied enthusiastically. "I'll get out on the streets today with some if you got 'em."

"No, I'm not interested in that. I want to sell 'em wholesale. Do you have anyone who can move large amounts?"

"Let me see what I can do," she said, thoroughly enjoying the high.

Two days later, she was on the phone. "Bobby, we can do business. Pick me up at Anacostia Avenue and 14th Street tomorrow afternoon at four o'clock. My man wants to talk to you."

This time Bobby flew down, boarding the plane with five bottles of Daladids in his briefcase. After the plane reached cruising altitude, he walked back to the bathroom. As he emerged from the bathroom he overheard someone say, "That looks like Reggie Jackson." It was true: Bobby Lloyd had a striking resemblance to the great ballplayer. To make matters worse, Bobby had unthinkingly donned a Yankees ball cap as he was leaving his apartment. By the time the plane was ready to land, it was abuzz with the fact that the superstar was in their midst.

The stewardess finally approached him. "Mr. Jackson," she whispered. "People are asking about the possibility of talking to you. I know you don't want to be bothered with this, so what we'd like to do is usher you off the plane as soon as we land. Someone will be waiting to get you through the airport, too," she added helpfully.

"Thank you so much," Bobby said, playing along with the charade. "I really don't need the attention right now."

Sure enough, when they landed, he was escorted through the airport and on to the rental car agency.

He was still chuckling over the incident when he picked up Keggie at the street corner. She directed him to drive a few blocks. "You can pull over right here," she said as they rounded a corner. "This is my connection's apartment. We can go on up there."

Bobby had known Keggie for years and trusted her; he wasn't so sure about her friends. They knocked at the door of the apartment and when no one answered, Keggie produced a key and let them in. The apartment was completely bare of furniture, leaving Bobby anxious about the situation. *Man, this feels like a rip-off. Why did I have to fly down*? He demanded of himself. *Now, I don't even have my piece with me.*

No, he reasoned. *There's no way Deborah would rip me off.*

In the meantime, she casually went to the refrigerator—the only thing in the place—and retrieved a bottle of water. *She ain't actin' like anything's happening*, Bobby told himself. *But this just don't feel right. They're gonna ice me, sure enough.*

"Keggie, where's your man?" he asked anxiously.

"He'll be here," she said nonchalantly.

I'm outta here, he told himself as his fears mounted. *I don't like this at all.*

You big punk, he scolded himself. *You always acting like the big man and the first little thing that don't seem normal you're ready to run!*

His inner turmoil was interrupted by a knock at the door. As Keggie let her connection in, Bobby noted with some relief that he was by himself. *Even if he's strappin', I'll take him down before he gets to his piece*, he assured himself.

"Bobby, this is Charles." The two dealers shook hands.

"I hear you got some D's," said Charles. "How much you want for 'em?"

"How much you willin' to pay?" Bobby retorted a little defensively.

"They're goin' for thirty bucks apiece on the streets," observed Charles. "I'll give you twenty-five hundred a jar."

"I'll tell you what, I'll sell them to you for two thousand bucks a bottle," said Bobby. It was worth giving the guy a good deal to be able to unload them easily. "How many can you take?"

"I can take whatever you got," Charles gushed.

"I got five jars with me."

"I'll be back in a few minutes," he said as he strode out the door.

He's gonna come back with some friends, Bobby thought. But all his fears were quieted when Charles showed up fifteen minutes later with $10,000 cash.

Bobby and his boys made repeated trips to Washington over the following months, until all the Daladids were gone. The two con men made hundreds of thousands of dollars on the scheme.

Yes, Bobby Lloyd was living large, but outward success does not always equate with inner contentment. He would soon discover that sin *always* comes at a price.

In Harlem

CHAPTER FIFTEEN

Live by the Sword, Die by the Sword

One frigid, clear evening in December 1975, Bobby slipped into the Lenox Lounge in Harlem, saddling a stool at the quiet end of the bar. "Horace, you seen Solomon tonight?" Bobby asked the middle-aged bartender.

Horace quickly glanced around to make sure no one could hear him. "Word is he's laying low. You ain't gonna see him around for awhile."

"Why, what's up?"

"You know Stanley Morgan?" he asked in a whisper.

"Yeah, I seen him around," said Bobby, leaning over the bar to hear better. Bobby's memory supplied an image of a man whose once-powerful frame had been wasted by years of heroin addiction.

"Well, word is the other night Solly walked into the Shalimar and sparked him with eight shots right at his table," announced the bartender.

"You're kiddin'," responded Bobby. He wasn't surprised to hear his boss had murdered someone, only that he had shot him in front of a bar full of witnesses.

"Yeah, but get this. He used a rifle!"

"A rifle!"

"Yeah, he walked in with a rifle under his overcoat and lit him up, walked out cool as could be. Clean and brutal."

"I heard Stanley was tight with Nicky Barnes," argued Bobby. "They were joined at the hip for years. He had to have okayed it."

"I hear the D.A. was leanin' on him and The Council was worried he was gonna flip."

"Yeah, he seemed kinda' soft, like he could be turned," speculated Bobby.

But ain't that the world I live in? Bobby thought to himself as he finished his drink. *Clean and brutal.* He took pride in the fact that his life had become more dangerous than ever. *Ain't many can handle this life*, he thought, congratulating himself. *Stan couldn't hang—too much for him. Dudes like that always go down.*

What Bobby didn't yet realize was that his life of crime was beginning to catch up to him as well. He had always been considered a standup guy: steady, reliable, willing to help his friends. But something evil was taking over inside him. Bobby Lloyd, who had always prided himself on his ability to control his passions and remain cool in the face of any kind of provocation or danger, was finding himself increasingly losing his composure.

One case in point is that of Kenny, who was granted a position as a low-level drug courier because he was married to Bobby's cousin. Kenny was a typical junkie, greedy to get his hands on heroin any time he could. This greed drove him to make two mistakes. First, he had stolen money he had received from street dealers that was supposed to be delivered back to Bobby. On top of that, it came out that he had been dipping into the quantities he was delivering. Bobby became furious when he found out that his dealers were under the impression that *he* was shortchanging them.

Bobby began looking for Kenny, determined to kill him. One day he was riding around Hempstead with Sandy, one of his side kicks, when he spotted the thief emerging from a bar. Bobby had her get in the backseat and pulled his Caddie alongside Kenny, now walking down the sidewalk.

"Yo, Kenny, come here!" Bobby hollered. The junkie froze, frantically looking for an escape route.

"Come here, man," Bobby continued in a more friendly tone. "I just wanna talk to you."

The junkie reluctantly slid into the front seat.

"I'm gonna ask you a question. Don't lie to me. You owe us money. And, on top of that, you been skimming off the top of the bags."

He didn't even get to the question before Kenny frantically poured forth a stream of denials. This was his third mistake because in Bobby's skewed sense of right-and-wrong, being lied to was intolerable. Bobby grabbed the .38 from his waistband and began beating him in the head with it, blood spurting from Kenny's ear. The thief screamed for mercy, which only increased Bobby's rage. "I'm gonna kill ya!" he yelled, taking aim at his head. By now Sandy was also screaming and when Bobby raised his gun, she impulsively grabbed it, pulling it backwards. Kenny took the opportunity to open his door and throw himself on the sidewalk. Bobby was going to shoot him right on the spot, but his hand had become ensnarled in the head rest and he couldn't aim it. Kenny scampered off, making good his escape.

Kenny wasn't the only one to take advantage of Bobby's trust. Ricky had gotten in the Drug Lord's good graces because he was involved with Dianne, Jack's younger sister. One sweltering summer afternoon, Bobby was driving through Lakeview when he noticed Ricky walking down the street. He looked all the part of a sick junkie: shirt disheveled, afro unkempt, nose running.

Always ready to be the guardian of the Jack family, Bobby pulled his car along the curb. "Ricky, what's wrong with you?"

"Oh, man, I'm sick," he sniveled. "I ain't gotten high since last night."

"Get in, I'll help ya out." Bobby never—never, ever—kept drugs on him when he was in public. Ricky's dilemma pressed him to break another of his cardinal rules: Don't ever bring anyone other than close, trustworthy friends to your home. Bobby drove Ricky to his Hempstead apartment. He gave him some dope and a few bucks to catch a bus and sent him on his way.

When Bobby came home that night, he discovered that someone had ransacked the place and had stolen some money, drugs and, worst of all, his favorite gun—a nickel-plated .32.

Ricky! *He's the only one it could have been*, Bobby raged.

He immediately put the word out on the streets that he would give $1,000 to anyone who would inform him of the thief's whereabouts. Bobby was determined to kill him.

About a week later, Bobby was driving through the Rockville Centre projects when he spotted Ricky getting into his Buick. As luck would have it, Bobby wasn't driving his Cadillac but a less conspicuous secondary car he kept for drug deals. He drove on by Ricky, pulled a U-turn at the end of the block and parked about thirty yards behind the Buick. He didn't have a gun with him, so he grabbed the Buck knife he kept in his glove box and quickly made his way up the street. Just as he got to the driver's door, he lunged toward the window. Ricky must have spotted him in the mirror at the last instant because he threw himself toward the passenger door just as Bobby's knife buried itself in the cloth-covered seat. As he struggled to extricate the blade, Ricky darted out the other door and ran for his life.

Bobby Lloyd, always the cool one, felt like he was falling apart inside. There is an old adage known among churchgoers who struggle with addictions: Sin will take you further than you ever wanted to go, keep you longer than you ever wanted to stay, and cost you more than you could ever pay. While it is true of addictions to drugs and sex, it is also true of other forms of sin.

Bobby's ability to maintain his composure had always been one of his greatest qualities. He had seen so many drug dealers arrested or even killed simply because they had gotten sloppy in their personal habits. Now he was the one who was emotionally unraveling.

Bobby now had five daughters by three different women. Loretta had given birth to his fifth and final child a daughter, Bobbette. He lived a double life juggling several different households and lady friends, leaving a string of children behind.

What he couldn't understand at this point of his life was that there is an irresistible trend with sin. Because of its corrupting influences upon a person's emotions and thinking, it always, always leads to errors in judgment. No one is exempt from this tendency.

While Bobby was becoming increasingly out of control with his behavior, he also was becoming less aware of what was happening around him. Indeed, he had come up on the radar of local law enforcement officials. Bobby Lloyd was about to be squeezed...

Heroin Ring Is Smashed, Police Say

By Bill Van Haintze
and T. J. Collins

Lakeview—Nassau Narcotic squad detectives rounded up eight members of an alleged Lakeview-Hempstead heroin-peddling ring yesterday that police said netted at least $3,000 a week in street sales. More arrests are expected.

Narcotic squad commander Otto Geiger said the ring, which had been under surveillance since July, was so cautious in its operations that undercover detectives were unable to set up a buy. Gieger described the ring as "a careful, close-knit group."

The leader of the ring was identified by police as Robert Lloyd, 30, an auto mechanic who lives at 182 N. Central Ave., Lakeview.

Police said Lloyd or one of the other ring members ... and Queens on an alternate weekly basis and brought it back to sell in Nassau County. Lloyd, police said, was clearing $1,000 a week from the operation for himself.

Lloyd was charged with conspiracy to possess and sell drugs, two counts of criminal possession of heroin, possession of a pistol and possession of marijuana and hypodermic needles.

A sawed-off shotgun was seized at the home of another suspect, Ulric Francis, 21, of 519 Coolidge Ave., Lakeview, police said. In addition to charges of possessing the weapon and conspiracy to possess and sell drugs, Francis also was accused of possessing a hypodermic needle and marijuana, police said.

Other members of the ring, who are all charged with conspiracy to possess and sell drugs, and the additional charges against them, according to police are: Edith Hughes, 37, of 380 Front St., Hempstead, possession of a .38-cal. revolver and possession of heroin; Joseph Harris, 30, possession of heroin and a hypodermic needle; Godfrey Monroe, 27, of the Coolidge

Avenue address, possession of a hypodermic needle; Keith Dunham, 27, of 417 Clinton Ave., Lakeview, a chemical salesman, illegal possession of Valium; Dandra Gill, 26, of 1187 Langdon Blvd., and Kevin Hurdle, 19, of 467 Clinton Ave., both of Lakeview.

Six of the defendants were arraigned yesterday in Nassau County Court, Mineola; the others are to be arraigned today. Dunham, Monroe and Hurdle each were held in $100,000 bail for hearings next week. Francis was held in $10,100 bail for a hearing Wednesday; Hughes in $101,000 for a hearing Tuesday, and Ms. Gill for $120,000 for a hearing Tuesday.

Newsday Photo by Dick Kraus

Five of the eight suspects arrested line up before police desk to be booked in Mineola

NEWSDAY, SATURDAY, APRIL 17, 1976

Heroine Ring Smashed 1976

Bobby is booked

Robert Lloyd is booked.

CHAPTER SIXTEEN

The Big Bust

As is typical of all good street cops, James Orlich had developed relationships with various low-lifes in his Lakeview precinct who would keep him abreast of what was happening on the streets. One of these snitches was Kenny, the man Bobby had beaten with his pistol. In July, 1975 Kenny told Officer Orlich that Bobby Lloyd was dealing heroin from his basement apartment located at 794 Woodfield Road. The cop dutifully sent a memo about it to the narcotics bureau.

Nathaniel Worthy, a 12-year veteran of the Nassau County Police Department, and his partner Stanley Mazyck were assigned to investigate the matter. It didn't take them long to conclude that this was no smalltime hood pushing a few dime bags of dope. This was a major drug ring being used to funnel the majority of the heroin entering Nassau County. They immediately contacted the local office of the Drug Enforcement Agency, which provided federal agents to assist in the investigation.

One of the first things the team learned about their antagonist was that he was extremely careful. Many drug dealers become so flamboyant in their activities that law enforcement officers find them relatively easy to arrest and convict. Bobby Lloyd was not only subdued in the clothes he wore, the cars he drove, and the lifestyle he led, but he was also exceptionally cautious about doing business with people he didn't know. Worthy and Mazyck knew that the only way they would snag this cagey criminal was through the combined use of surveillance, telephone taps, and informants.

For several months the house "was intermittently kept under surveillance" by Worthy and Mazyck. They "observed vehicles owned by other individuals, also suspected of dealing in controlled substances" visiting the premises on different occasions. [11]

Bobby lived with a girl named Sandy Bass at the apartment. A number of dealers were allowed access to the place, but most of its traffic was from the members of Bobby's crew: Kevin, John, Ricky, and Godfrey. As time went on, all of these players were routinely tailed and eventually their residences were staked out as well.

The detectives eventually presented their findings to the district attorney's office, which was able to secure court ordered wiretaps on the telephones of all Bobby's crew. From the beginning it was obvious that those who spoke on the phone were being extremely guarded in their communications, but little blurbs were picked up by the investigators: Kevin telling Brad that he had "a half" and that Brad should "hold it;" a deal worked out in obscure terms with a man named Roger; a woman named Betty complaining "about the weight in quarters she had bought" from Bobby; and finally, a man named Solomon arranging for Bobby to pick up a quantity of "product" in Manhattan.

All of this information was helpful to put together a case of conspiracy to sell drugs, but it was all circumstantial evidence. The detectives decided to utilize informants in the investigation. Two separate informants attempted to purchase drugs from Bobby to no avail. Worthy and Mazyck needed someone Bobby knew, and they just happened to have a snitch "in their back

---

11   Application for Eavesdropping Warrant by the Nassau County District Attorney's Office.

pocket" who had known Bobby since childhood but ten years his senior, Dave, a small time numbers runner who was hooked on heroine but had some good contacts. Stan began to hang out at a couple of joints Bobby frequented and the two renewed their friendship.

One night in January, 1976, Dave called Bobby from the Pot Belly Pub in West Hempstead. Standing alongside him were the two detectives.

"Bobby, this is Dave."

"What's up, man?"

"Hey I'm in need tonight. You mind if I stop by?"

"Uh, yeah, okay, come on by."

Dave drove over to Woodfield Road with the $30 the detectives had given him. Bobby took his money but wouldn't give him drugs himself. "Listen, I want you to go to 525 Coolidge Avenue and park your car in front. Kevin will come out and give you three dimes." Dave did what he was told and immediately took the dope Kevin had given him to the detectives. They confirmed it was heroin with a field test. They now had Bobby taking the money from an informant, but they needed more than that.

The other challenge was that the snitches were fearful. An officer wrote in his search warrant application, "These informants would be unwilling to testify at trial as they fear that if identified, they will be killed by individuals connected with Lloyd. Informant no. 3 has further informed me that Bobby Lloyd is often armed with a .32 caliber revolver." [12]

Meanwhile, as part of the investigation, DEA agents were able to successfully purchase drugs from Ricky, one of Bobby's four main crew members. He had four ounces of heroin in his

12 Application for a Search Warrant submitted by Nathaniel Worthy to Judge Bernard Tomson.

possession when they picked him up. It was this arrest that sent Bobby to Solomon looking for more drugs. [13] DEA agents noted Bobby's visit to the club but chose not to attempt an arrest at that time.

On April 15, 1976, Bobby arranged for Lee and Sandy, one of Bobby's women, to pick up a quantity of heroin from one of Solomon's men in Queens. When they returned to Hempstead, to Edy's crib, another one of Bobby's women, they spent several hours cutting and packaging it. Bobby met one of his regular dealers at a local bar and gave him the entire package.

Bobby and Sandy were sound asleep at the apartment on Woodfield Road early the next morning when an enormous boom jolted them awake. Bobby's first thought was that someone was trying to rip him off, so he grabbed the .38 from under his pillow and jumped out of bed. For some inexplicable reason, Sandy kicked the gun out of his hand, just a split second before members of the local SWAT team burst through the bedroom door. Had that gun still been in his hand, there's little doubt that he would have been shot dead on the spot.

The groggy couple was allowed to dress before being handcuffed. It just so happened that the pants Bobby grabbed had a gram of pure heroin in the pocket. The couple sat on the couch as the police ransacked their basement apartment. *I gotta figure out how to get rid of this stuff*, Bobby fretted. Suddenly he got an inspiration. "Officer, I gotta go to the bathroom!"

The detective un-cuffed him and led him to the bathroom, leaving the door ajar. "Officer, this ain't right. I need some privacy," he complained. The cop handcuffed him to the sink and closed the door. The prisoner took the opportunity to snort the powder, emerging from the bathroom light-headed and clearly out of sorts.

---

13 See Prologue.

"Are you okay?" asked the cop.

"Oh, I'm fine now, officer," Bobby responded cheerfully.

A little while later, one of the detectives picked up Bobby's telephone. "Woodfield Road is secure," he said, without even dialing another number; indicating Bobby's phone had been tapped.

"What's happening at Front Street?"

"Uh huh, alright, let us know what you find," said the cop to the officer at the other location.

"Coolidge Avenue, are you on the line?" he asked.

"You did, huh? Okay, just keep us in the loop," continued the one-sided conversation.

Two hours later, the couple was taken to police headquarters in Mineola where they joined Ricky, Kevin, Lee, and three others who had been arrested. They were all booked for conspiracy to sell narcotics. According to the arrest report, several weapons, a number of small packets of heroin, an assortment of ammunition, syringes, and drug packaging paraphernalia were confiscated.

Considering it had been an eight-month investigation, the police had little to show for their efforts. However, thanks to the Rockefeller Law enacted two years prior, the district attorney's office knew that if they could convict the defendants for the sale of narcotics, they could all be sentenced to life in prison.

For the next seven months the eight conspirators languished in jail as the case ground through the judicial system. Eventually, the district attorney approached Bobby's lawyer about the possibility of a plea agreement. Bobby insisted that the others be spared prison time. This wasn't out of the question since they didn't have arrest records. His lawyer pressed for one more concession. Instead of a fixed life sentence without possibility of parole, he requested that they amend the sentence to insert the phrase "one year to" life in prison. Bobby could still end up spending the rest of his natural life behind bars, but this small addition at least afforded the possibility of a release on parole one day.

On December 1, 1976, Bobby stood before the Honorable Judge Bernard Tomson for sentencing. "Robert Lloyd, you have been found guilty of conspiracy to sell and distribute narcotics. For your crimes against the people of New York, I sentence you to imprisonment for one year to life. You are to be remanded to the Department of Corrections for immediate transport to Sing Sing Correctional Facility."

Doing time in prison
1976

Sing Sing Prison

CHAPTER SEVENTEEN

Sing Sing

Sing Sing. The very name elicited awe and fear on the streets. To be sent "up the river" or to "the big house" were phrases coined in reference to this notorious prison perched along the banks of the Hudson River. Its 150-year history had seen the worst that New York had to offer, including old-time gangsters such as Mafia godfather Lucky Luciano and Lepke Buchalter, founder of Murder, Inc.

As he sat in his Nassau County jail cell awaiting transfer, Bobby contemplated the reality of spending the rest of his life in such a place. *I should just kill myself,* he thought, looking at the bars in front of him. *I could rip this sheet into strips and make a rope...*But as quickly as the suicidal inspiration came, it left. *What am I thinking? I ain't goin' down that easy. I'll find a loophole or somethin'.*

The next morning Bobby was shackled and herded with a handful of other inmates into a Department of Corrections bus. The convicts sat silently as the bus lurched forward into Long Island traffic. Jive talk and frivolity was noticeably absent, every man a prisoner of his own fear-plagued imagination. The trip was surprisingly short. As the bus approached the infamous penitentiary, the first thing that stood out to Bobby was the fifteen-foot high brick wall, upon which a chain link fence stood, crowned with several runs of barbed wire. Octagonal guard towers loomed along the wall every hundred feet or so. The immensity of the brick barrier overwhelmed one's senses.

The bus stopped momentarily at the gate before proceeding to the receiving unit. The arriving inmates were marched into the building, where they were stripped of their clothes, forced to endure a humiliating orifice check, showered, and provided a new uniform.

The new inmates were then paraded through the cell block that would become their home. Bobby's cell was on the third of four tiers. As he walked down the catwalk, he could feel the evaluating stares of the inmates in the cells he passed, each halting all personal activity for the welcome relief of something new to observe. Being a "fish" in a maximum-security prison like Sing Sing is an intimidating experience for anyone—even those who had been tough on the streets.

The guard opened the cell door allowing Bobby access. *Man, I'm just glad I got a cell to myself,* he thought as he scanned his new home. It couldn't have been more than six feet wide and eight feet long. The bed was a gray piece of metal extending from the right-side wall, its outer corners upheld by chains stretched at a 45º angle, mounted to the same wall. On it lay a piece of two-inch foam rubber encased in tattered green plastic, which served as a mattress. On the floor in the back of the cell squatted a formidable metal commode. Next to it a tiny sink jutted out of the left-side wall, over which hung a square piece of polished tin, prison's imitation of a mirror. His view was limited to the catwalk and its handrails, covered with multiple layers of institutional gray paint. The wall beyond it offered windows that provided light diffused by years of encrusted dust and grime. A stench of nicotine—old and rancid—permeated everything in the building.

Bobby had just gotten settled into his new digs when suddenly his cell door—along with the rest of the doors on the tier—unexpectedly clanged open. He stepped out of his cell, filing in line with the other prisoners, and marched to the chow hall. His column joined ranks with a larger line of inmates on the main floor. Soon the procession entered a vast, noisy auditorium, crammed with at least a hundred eight-foot steel tables holding a thousand prisoners or more. The line progressed along the serving counter. Bobby carefully mimicked the movements of the men in front of him. Within a minute his tray had received its ladle of slop, a piece of stale white bread, a chocolate chip cookie and a half pint of milk.

He sat down at the first available table, warily checking out its residents. *Nobody better try to snatch any of my food*, Bobby announced to himself, having viewed too many exaggerated prison movies. In his mind, everyone knew he was a fish, but the reality was that no one paid any attention to him. After rushing through his meal, he hurried out of the place, anxious for the security of his own cell.

That evening the cell doors once again clanged open, bringing forth the same line of inhabitants. "What's up, man? Where we goin' now?" Bobby asked his neighbor, feeling a little more confident.

"This is rec time," his tier-mate answered. "You'll see."

Bobby remained suspicious of everyone. Once again, the line joined the greater procession on the lower level. This time the men massed into a different assembly hall. As Bobby warily eyed his surroundings, he suddenly heard a voice cry out above the clamor. "Yo, homey! Bobby!" He turned around to see Frank, sent up earlier for selling his heroin. Relief swept over him at the sight of someone he knew. Frank maneuvered his way over to his boss and the two embraced. "Man, it's good to see ya," gushed Bobby uncharacteristically.

"Oh, I'm glad to see you, too," countered Frank, putting his arm around Bobby's shoulders. "I heard you were comin'."

Just then another friend approached. "Hey, Bobby, what's happenin'?" No sooner had he started talking to him then another four acquaintances walked up. Within the hour, he had seen twenty guys he knew from the streets. Over the next few days, as word spread that he was there, guys he didn't even know approached him. Bobby Lloyd had to get sent to Sing Sing to discover how widespread his reputation had become on the streets of New York.

****

A reputation helped, but it was no guarantee a guy could escape his stint in prison unharmed. One never knew what might happen. Sometimes men came to blows without a moment's notice. The possibility of violence was enough to keep an inmate alert, but on top of that was the ever-present danger from armed guards. For instance, if a fight broke out on the yard, the loudspeaker would announce, "Lockdown on the yard." That was a warning to stop right where you were and sit down on the ground. Correctional officers would immediately level their high-powered rifles at the area of disturbance.

Even more dangerous was the chow hall where guards armed with shotguns stalked a catwalk fifteen feet above the floor. If a disturbance broke out in there, tear gas canisters would be launched into the middle of the auditorium. If that didn't quell the violence, the officers had the authority to shoot. Anyone standing near the combatants could easily be shot.

One evening Bobby was marching along in line with the others when two young blacks began arguing with each other.

Their heated words brought instant tension into the line. Bobby knew better than to try to intervene. Yet, at the same time, he knew if they started fighting he could get shot as well.

Just then another brother confronted the main combatant. "Yo man, if you don't shut up, I'll stick a shiv right in ya! You wanna deal wit' him, deal wit' him outside the chow line. 'Cause if I get tear-gassed, I'll take you outta here."

Argument ended. *Wow, that was good*, Bobby smiled, appreciating the man's decisiveness.

****

One hot summer day, Bobby and an old con were sitting in the shade provided by the brick wall surrounding the yard. They were casually chatting when suddenly a long agonizing cry, full of pathos, pierced the clamor of the inmate population. For an eternal moment all the loud-mouthing and jive-talking ceased and an eerie stillness overtook the yard.

"What was *that*?" whispered Bobby to his older friend.

"Dat's da Wail, man," he replied. "That dude just got hit with his reality—he's gonna spend the rest of his life in this place. You hear it occasionally," he added nonchalantly.

Bobby's eyes scanned the yard, locking onto the source of the plaintiff cry. The kid couldn't have been more than 22 years old.

"You know what, Bobby?" the old con continued. "If the wrong man heard that today, that kid could get turned tonight."

"Why's that?" questioned Bobby.

"Cause he just showed weakness. For instance, look across the yard over there. You see that giant, ugly as sin, over there?" he asked, nodding in the direction of a hulking black man standing near the baseball diamond. "That's Mama Dear. If he decides he wants that kid, he'll take him. If the dude can't fight him off, he'll make him his woman."

"How'd he get a name like that?" asked Bobby.

"I dunno. Why don't you go ask him?" the old man teased, a grin creasing his wrinkled face. "You always gotta watch your back in this place, youngblood," he added ominously.

Bobby grimly nodded his head, grateful for the lesson.

CHAPTER EIGHTEEN

Downstate

One day, an officer read a list of prison identification numbers, including Bobby's, over the loudspeaker. "Roll up your belongings and report to admin." Such an announcement meant those inmates were either being released or transferred to another facility.

"You're going to Woodbourne, Lloyd," the guard at the office told him. Later that same day, he was being assigned a cell in his new home. *This is alright*, Bobby told himself as he checked out the medium security facility.

The atmosphere in Woodbourne was unquestionably more relaxed. Bobby had become so accustomed to the tension filling the air at Sing Sing that it took a few weeks for him to relax. Even the correctional officers were more laid back.

"Hey Lloyd," yelled a turnkey one afternoon.

Bobby emerged from his cell and walked to the guard's desk. "What's up, Officer Kyle?"

"Hey, can I check out this *Penthouse* magazine before I give it to you?"

"How'd I get that in here?" queried Bobby.

"Well, if you had a subscription before you entered the system, they have to give it to you."

Bobby had a long history of womanizing. In any given week, he could easily end up in bed with seven different women. That sexual lust now found its attention turned on the airbrushed images found in girlie magazines. As luck would have it, he was the only prisoner at Woodbourne receiving each month's issue of *Penthouse*. As the word got around that he had copies of the cherished publication, guys started dropping by asking to borrow them. Bobby immediately saw an opportunity to capitalize on the situation.

"Yo, Bobby, let me get one of those magazines," announced Willie, a chubby, likeable character from Buffalo.

"Sure, Willie, but it's gonna cost ya'," responded Bobby, handing him a copy. "Find a page you want and tell me what you'll gimme for it."

Willie perused the glossy pages until he landed on one that struck his fancy. "I'll give you five cigarettes for this one," said he, trying to sound generous.

"That page there? That'll cost you a half a pack," retorted Bobby.

"Man, you drive a hard bargain," complained Willie as he handed Bobby his half-pack of Kools.

The magazines became so popular, there were actually some evenings that guys would line up at his cell to work a deal with him.

****

Everyone looked forward to Saturday mornings because all of the cells were opened up, allowing free movement throughout the four tiers. Bobby was standing at his sink shaving when he heard some thumping noises and what sounded like a faint cry coming from down his tier.

He stepped out of his cell and saw that a scuffle was under way in another cell. He ran there to find two blacks wrestling with a pint-sized Hispanic. Bobby grabbed the bigger of the two by his collar, heaving him out of the cell. Then he punched the other guy in the back of the head. "Yo, man, this ain't none a yer business," the man responded, rising up to meet his challenger.

"I'm makin' it my business," retorted Bobby.

By now the fracas had gained the attention of inmates and guards alike. "I'll deal with you later," the black guy yelled as he and his partner ran off.

Bobby offered his hand to the kid sprawled halfway on his bunk. "Those dudes were trying to rape me, man. Thanks for helping me," he said, pulling himself upright with Bobby's help.

Moments later several guards arrived. "What's going on here, Lloyd?" demanded the first on the scene.

"I dunno. Two black guys were beating this kid up and I pulled them off him," said Bobby, straightening out his disheveled shirt. He purposely hid the sexual aspect of the assault.

"That's alright, we know who they were," remarked the guard.

That evening a middle-aged brother sat down next to Bobby in the chow hall. "Listen Bobby, I need to let you know that there's a hit out on you. Apparently you interfered with some dudes who are connected. Watch yer back, youngblood."

The word was that the two attackers were members of a loose-knit black prison gang. They were immediately shipped off to another facility, but they still had plenty of friends at Woodbourne.

The following day Bobby walked up to the weight bench. He had become part of a racially diverse group that worked out together everyday. "Bobby, I heard about what happened," said Ricardo, a powerfully built Puerto Rican from South Bronx. "Listen, we gotch yer back, man."

"Yeah, man, we're watchin' out for ya," added Simon, a brother from Albany. All his weight-lifting buddies—Spanish, whites, and African-Americans—assured him they were looking out for him.

A few nights later, Bobby was walking down a darkened hallway that connected the commissary to his tier. "It's only a matter a time, nigger," snarled an ominous voice from the shadows. Bobby kept on walking, but it was a good reminder that he needed to be careful.

About a month later, a Mexican-American inmate approached Bobby in the yard. "You're Bobby Lloyd." It was a statement of fact, not a question.

"Yeah, what's up?"

"Armando wants to talk to you." Having delivered his message, he turned around and walked away. Bobby knew Armando was recognized as the leader of the Spanish population. *I wonder what he wants with me*, Bobby thought. *There's only one way to find out.* He followed the young Latino to the other side of the yard where Armando sat at a picnic table, a group of intimidating Hispanics gathered around him. In prison, it is understood that you never approach such a group uninvited.

Bobby sauntered up to the table, doing his best to hide his apprehension.

"Listen, man," began the leader. "We appreciate what you did for our little brother. It took a lot of guts to cross that line and stick up for him. We want you to come to our festival next week." The others offered welcoming smiles as Armando addressed him.

"Yeah man, I'll be there."

Bobby walked away surprised by the offer. Woodbourne allowed each major racial group to hold a festival once a year. During their respective days, they had the yard all to themselves and their families.

The following week Bobby attended the festivities; the only black man ever to do so. The appreciation the Hispanics felt toward him didn't end there, either. From that day on, a delicious dish of Spanish cuisine was delivered to his cell twice a week. Bobby was grateful for their gesture, but he was still a marked man.

Not long after the Spanish festival, he was approached on the yard by an inmate whom he readily recognized as a leader of the black population.

"Yo, Bobby Lloyd," the menacing brother said as he walked up. Bobby immediately began sizing up the situation, looking around to see if there were either friends or foes nearby. "Listen, we didn't like what you did with the brothers, but we dig it. It's over. Don't worry about it," he said, walking away. His statements were given with the authority of one in charge.

If Bobby had any lingering doubts, they were squelched the following week at the Black festival. He wondered if he would get the cold shoulder from his brothers in that setting, but just the opposite seemed to be the case. Different ones approached him, making him feel as though he were part of the family. *It really is over*, he told himself with much relief.

****

"Bobby, did you hear about Nicky Barnes?" Bobby Lloyd turned around to see Lewis walking up to him. Lewis was an old acquaintance from Queens.

"What's happenin'?" asked Bobby, scanning the yard to see who could hear what would be said. Bobby knew the DEA had made a huge bust a few months prior to this, arresting Nicky, Solomon and more than twenty other guys as well. This wasn't anything to be necessarily alarmed about considering the high-powered attorneys those guys retained. Somehow Nicky Barnes' lawyer always managed to get him acquitted of his charges.

"*New York Times Magazine* did an article on him," said Lewis, trying to catch his breath. "He posed in a suit, lookin' all arrogant. And get this, the caption says, 'Mr. Untouchable' in big, bold print."

"Wow, that's not good," responded Bobby.

"Yeah, well, that ain't all. President Carter saw the picture and got ticked. He put the word out to bring Nicky Barnes down no matter what."

"Wow," Bobby repeated. "Man, that dude's crazy! Why'd he pose for a picture like that?"

"The way I hear it is they told him that if he didn't pose in a suit, they were gonna use this dreadful lookin' mug shot of him on the cover. So I guess he figured if they're gonna do a story on him, he mize well look good for it."

It was the beginning of the end for Nicky Barnes and his organization. A few months later, he was convicted on conspiracy to sell drugs and sentenced to life in prison. Perhaps he could have endured this, but in the coming years, the other members of The Council squandered the organization he had labored to build. The final slap in his face was when he discovered that one of his partners was sleeping with his woman. Nicky Barnes got his revenge by turning state's evidence against all of his former associates.

Of course, the entire scope of this organizational collapse was unknown to Bobby Lloyd at this point. Nevertheless, once the kingpin was convicted and sentenced to life, Bobby knew that, should he ever get released, there would be no Nicky Barnes crime family to work for. He would be on his own.

Dianne & Daddy the day of Gregory's christening

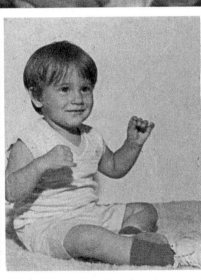

Dianne and baby Gregory

CHAPTER NINETEEN

A Surrendered Life

While Bobby languished in prison, day after day repeating the same monotonous routine, he had no idea that a visit from an old friend was about to change his whole life.

It would be an understatement to say that the early '70s had not been kind to Dianne Jack, now a divorced mother. In fact, she was in a prison of her own, spending most of her time each day scheming, stealing, or somehow earning enough money for the next fix. Each morning when she awoke, already feeling sick and on edge, the process started all over again. Every other aspect of her life was pushed into the background by the ever demanding demon of heroin attached to her mind.

Dianne lived in Rockville Centre, but a lot of her time was spent in the shooting galleries of Harlem or the Lower East Side of Manhattan. Somehow in the midst of this hellish living she successfully completed beauty school, but her addiction often caused her to miss work, and when she *was* there, she would sometimes nod out while working on some poor woman's hair! It also caused her to give up custody of five-year-old Gregory, her precious son whom she dearly loved, to his paternal grandmother.

By 1974, Dianne Jack was a walking corpse. Her wild blond hair only accentuated her gaunt appearance. She was constantly sick, constantly in need of a fix. Her arms were covered with track marks, abscesses and ulcers. She had shot up so many times in her left arm that there was a festering sore over the primary vein.

She didn't even need to puncture the skin to get a good hit in that hole.

To further exacerbate her frustration, it seemed as though every time she went to cop dope, there were Christians waiting to tell her that she needed Jesus. *These people are out of their minds*, she would tell herself. But she couldn't seem to escape them. One Hispanic girl in particular, named Laura, always seemed to find her, pressing her to give her life to the Lord. Dianne felt sorry for them for believing such junk and ignored all of them.

One day in 1975, she was particularly frustrated and out of sorts. Very sick, and needing desperately to get high, she cooked up the heroin as usual but was unable to hit a vein. Although she tried several times, her veins were collapsed!

Hoping to escape her mental agitation, she turned on her television. *The 700 Club* was airing so she got up to change the channel. Pat Robertson's words stopped her in her tracks. "If you're addicted to heroin, I want to pray with you right now," he said. "Just get on your knees and repeat this prayer after me." Through gritted teeth, Dianne repeated the prayer. Unfortunately, nothing seemed to change. The merry-go-round of finding money and getting high continued unabated.

One day about three weeks later, she had to take her parents to a family service clinic hoping they would be able to get off the assortment of psychotropic drugs they had become addicted to. The first step in the process was to undergo an interview by a social worker named Don. After they were done, the man asked to speak to Dianne privately. "You're a junkie," he said, pointing at the track marks on her hands. "You can get clean if you want to."

She was taken aback by his forwardness and denied it. "What do you know about it, anyway?"

"I used to have a hundred-dollar-a-day habit," he said. "But I've been clean for ten years now."

Now he had her attention. "How'd you get clean?" she asked.

"I went through a two-year program at Day Top," he stated matter-of-factly. "Listen, if you're serious about kicking the habit, I can help you get in."

Years of street life had left her cynical, but the more he talked, the more hopeful she felt. Over the next two weeks, the two were in constant contact by telephone. Finally, Don called with good news. "Dianne, there's an opening in the program," he told her. "But I've got some bad news. The report came back from your tests: You have hepatitis B. Your liver and kidneys are in the process of shutting down. You need to go to the hospital for treatment and then you gotta get de-toxed."

She was put in isolation for a week, then a seven-day Detox Unit of St. John's Hospital as the white poison worked itself out of her system. A daily dose of Methadone helped her survive the withdrawal period. Bobby heard from the Jack family. Once again, they informed him, Dianne was in the hospital in detox. Concerned for this life-long friend, he got a call through making sure she was okay and relieved that she may finally make it out of these mean streets. Little did they know, both of their lives were about to make an abrupt turn.

Once she completed that process, she was admitted into the "therapeutic community." It was an intense two-year program requiring patients to work through a series of psycho-therapeutic procedures. Every day there was a regimen of classes, group meetings, and personal counseling. The program relied heavily upon behavioral modification techniques.

One of the premises of the program was that unhealthy relationships the drug addicts maintained with certain family members and acquaintances contributed to their dependence on drugs. Part of the process of beginning a new life was to limit or even cut off all such relationships.

Past street friends were marked as dangerous. "Dianne," her counselor asked her in an early session, "is there anyone you have been involved with in the past that you still have a relationship with?"

Dianne crinkled up her forehead as she searched her memory. "Only Bobby Lloyd," she said, explaining their relationship, certain that her counselor would see the innocence of the friendship.

"You have to write him a letter informing him that you won't ever be seeing him again," the psychotherapist said, putting her pen on the desk.

This was a tough one to swallow for Dianne. "You don't understand," she argued. "Ever since I was a little girl he had my back and my family's. My relationship with him has been almost totally positive. He was the family protector and my protector in the street! To lump him in with the other men I've been with isn't fair."

"Dianne, you have to decide if you want to do this program. The bottom line is that all street relationships must be ended. I know it seems harsh, but we know what we're doing."

"I don't know..."

"Dianne, this man is a drug dealer. The very fact that you have always looked up to him is all the more reason why you must end it. I want you to write a letter and bring it to me this afternoon. I'll read it and send it off for you."

Dianne didn't want to do it, but she knew that she had to obey the rules or risk being expelled. Her life was on the line. She wrote the letter.

Her next hurdle was when they forbade her from having any contact with her family. She had to write them a letter as well, informing them that she couldn't have contact with them while in the program. They were furious when they received the letter, and several of them stormed off to the facility intent on rescuing her. The administrator attempted to explain the situation, but they weren't having it. Jimmy, Dianne's youngest sibling, got so angry he punched the poor man in the mouth.

Dianne was in her room and could hear the commotion. She desperately wanted to leave with them, but she knew death was waiting for her outside that facility. Tears streamed down her cheeks as she listened to the fracas in the reception area.

Several weeks later, she overheard a news report on the dayroom television describing a huge heroin ring that had been broken up in Nassau County. She arrived at the TV in time to see Bobby being ushered handcuffed into the police station. *Oh man*, she thought, *he's finished now.*

Dianne had showed such determination to have the freedom she saw in Don that she completed the two-year program in ten months.

Upon her return to Rockville Centre, she went about establishing a new life for herself: job, apartment, and different friends. She began restoring her relationship with her son now 8. I *will never go back to that life again*, she would regularly tell herself. The hell of it was still very real to her. Her efforts paid off for the next few years, but she noticed that the emotional pain in her heart was ever so present. She also missed her family.

She decided she needed to talk to her mentor about it. "Don," she began, "I did everything the community told me to do and I've been clean nearly three years. But I have one question for you. When does the emotional pain stop?"

"Oh that," he said, nodding his head knowingly. "You'll get used to that."

When Dianne heard that, she came completely undone. She had assumed that being clean meant she would become a happy person. "I'll never get used to that," she snapped, as she brushed by him.

On the way home, she actually panicked. Suicide seemed the only way. She devised a well thought out plan because she could not live like this anymore! But then she remembered the Hispanic girl who used to always tell her about this Jesus of hers. And then she thought of the time she gave her heart to the Lord in front of the television set. All of that seemed so distant now, so unattainable.

Life seemed so futile, so meaningless. Hopelessness seemed to engulf her. *What is the point of going on*? Throughout the day her emotions were tugged back and forth between thoughts of suicide and the memory of Laura. It had been two years since she had seen her. *I wonder if I could find her*, she thought, climbing into her '74 Volkswagen. A little while later she pulled along a curb in the girl's neighborhood, asking people about the girl who's always talking about Jesus.

"Oh, her! She lives on the next block," a lady said, shaking her head in disgust. Dianne found the apartment. Laura was happy to see her, but she was getting ready to attend a midweek church service. While Laura got ready, Dianne brought her up to date on all that had happened to her. "Laura, I need this Jesus you're always talkin' about," she told her, weeping. "I can't do this anymore!"

"You speak Spanish," said Laura. "You can go to church with me!"

On their way to the tiny Pentecostal church, Dianne kept asking what she needed to do.

"You'll see when you get there," was all the girl would tell her.

The pastor preached his heart out that Wednesday evening and, as he concluded, Laura urged her to go to the altar for prayer. Dianne didn't know exactly what to say to God, but she offered up a disjointed prayer of surrender. This time she really meant what she was saying. She was done running her own life. She wept away years of bitterness and pain. The hole that had been in her heart was instantly filled with Another. Somehow she knew that the Creator of the universe was living within her. The despair and thoughts of suicide were gone. She also knew that the days of stringently adhering to the rules and controls of the therapeutic community were over. She was free inside and would never again return to drugs.

As she drove home that night she knew she had to tell her family about what had happened to her. In fact, she couldn't wait for the opportunity. And she also knew she had to tell Bobby Lloyd.

A New Start for Bobby

Bobby at Grandma Mary's with Cheryl's daughters; Monique & Dawn

CHAPTER TWENTY

The Prison Door is Open

Perhaps it was one of those ironies of life that Ricky and Dianne's sister moved near Woodbourne, taking up residence just a short distance from the man who had once tried to avenge himself by stabbing Ricky while he sat in his car. But, of course, Bobby was locked away in a world unto itself, populated by men with an entirely different value system and pecking order than that of the outside community. Although he lived in close proximity, Ricky no longer feared Bobby Lloyd, for walls and chain link fencing kept him safely sequestered from society.

Dianne, in the exuberance so typical of new believers, was anxious to share her miracle with all of her loved ones. She was happier still to discover that she could "kill two birds with one stone" by driving up to Woodbourne, timing her trip to coincide with prison visiting hours.

Perhaps it was because he hadn't been near a woman in two years, but Bobby was taken aback by Dianne's restored beauty. The unmistakable smell of death had lingered about her the last time he had seen her. It would be a mistake to say she was back to her old self, for her physical beauty had matured and, more importantly, there was a freshness, a vitality, a beaming joy emanating from her that he had never before seen in a person.

"Hi, Dianne," Bobby said warmly, as she approached him in the visiting room. "It's so good to see you."

"It's good to see you too, Bobby," she responded cheerily.

"Man, you look great," he exclaimed. "You're outta the grave. How'd you do it?"

Dianne told Bobby the whole story: how her addiction had taken her to death's door, how she had entered the therapeutic community and started a new life but, still lacking joy, had found it in Jesus at a Pentecostal church. "Bobby, I've never known such happiness!"

The con was genuinely happy for her, but that didn't mean he was interested in her religion. He *was* interested in her, however, and decided that he could put up with her Christianity if it meant more visits.

Over the following weeks, Dianne dutifully made the drive to Woodbourne numerous times, but eventually quit coming when she realized that her efforts to win Bobby and her sister to Christ weren't paying off.

****

Meanwhile, Bobby met a white inmate named Brian Fielding, a man who would prove to have a dramatic effect on his life. Brian was a judge's son with a college education. During the course of prison life, he and Bobby became friends.

By the late '70s, the New York penal system had become stretched to the point of breaking. Sociologists working for the State conceived of a plan they believed would help paroled inmates successfully reenter society. This, in turn, would hopefully relieve overcrowded prisons. One of the interesting features of the program was that it would be operated by a team of inmates and recent college graduates.

Woodbourne Correctional Facility was chosen to host this grand experiment. And when the authorities came looking for an inmate to head up this effort, who better than the educated son of a judge?

So it was that Brian Fielding was chosen to lead the program. He, in turn, picked out four other inmates to join his team. His friend Bobby Lloyd was at the top of that list. A handful of college grads rounded out the team and they immediately got to work.

Brian's team had a genuine concern for the inmates they were processing. They did everything possible to help the men get jobs, find adequate housing, and make a respectable life for themselves on the outside. To the surprise of State officials, the program worked beautifully. Even the governor became excited about its success.

The correctional staff, however, did not share in the excitement of the State bureaucrats. They did not appreciate the fact that certain inmates were granted special privileges, such as use of telephones and so on.

Whether or not this accounted for the sudden parole of Brian Fielding and his team will likely never be known. Nevertheless, in December 1978 a shocked Bobby Lloyd stepped out of prison a free man.

Prison officials offered him a new set of clothes, but he wanted his own clothes back—the ones he had been wearing when he was arrested: a flashy gold shirt, bellbottom pants, and platform shoes. His brother Stevie was outside the main gate waiting for him and drove him back to Rockville Centre where family and friends were awaiting his arrival.

Bobby stepped out of the car beaming with pride over his "accomplishment." He felt like a giant as he confidently strode toward the crowd of family members and loved ones. But, to his surprise, people started giggling when they saw him. One of his friends finally exclaimed, "Bobby, what's up which you, man?"

"What chu talkin' about?" Bobby asked puzzled.

"Look at chu!" he said, pointing at him.

"What chu wanna look at?" Bobby asked, still clueless.

"Look at those pants and shoes. Platform shoes went out last year, man," he exclaimed with a tone of mock irritation. "And what's up with those bellbottoms, man?"

By now everyone was laughing and making fun of him. It was all good natured, but Bobby was still properly embarrassed. He turned to his brother, "Stevie, why didn't you tell me?"

"I didn't wanna say nothin'." Who was he to correct his older brother?

"Thanks a lot, bro!"

****

Bobby's first order of business was to get himself re-established. He had left substantial amounts of cash with various people he trusted, but when he went to retrieve it, most of it had been spent. "Man, Bobby, you know how it is," whined his cousin. "When we heard you got life, we figured you weren't comin' back." Still, he scraped enough together to buy himself a car, some clothes and, most importantly, some product. He was soon back in business.

One day Bobby drove to the Rockville Centre projects to visit two of his daughters. By this time their mother Cheryl was shacking up with Dave—the very man who had set Bobby up to get arrested. But this was information he wouldn't be privy to for many years. And Bobby had long since gotten over any territorial feelings he had. He was just checking to see if his girls were being taken care of because he had heard their mother was using.

He pulled his Cadillac onto the street encircling the cluster of apartment buildings and noticed two white men standing on the sidewalk in front of Cheryl's apartment talking to one of his daughters. *What are these dudes doin' talkin' to my little girl?* he fumed. Then he saw one of them hand her something..

"Yo, Dawn, what chu got there?" Bobby yelled, angrily getting out of his car.

"It's candy, Daddy," responded the ten-year-old.

"Give him back the candy," Bobby said.

"But Daddy..."

"I said give him back the candy," Bobby stated more forcefully.

"Who are you guys?" Bobby asked, turning to the two white guys.

"We're here with Dave," one responded.

"I don't care who you're with. If I ever see you guys give anything to any black kids in this neighborhood, I'll have your head," threatened Bobby.

"Do you know who you're talking to?" the man asked. The man didn't speak with anger, but there was definitely authority in his voice.

All this was lost on Bobby, who was still hot. "I don't care who you are. That's my daughter you just gave candy to. And if I see it again, guess what? You're gonna have some problems."

"Are you sure you know who you're talking to?" The man was maintaining his composure but was beginning to get irritated by this upstart.

By now Dave emerged from the apartment. The other guy was talking now. "This brother's giving us some trouble."

"Bobby, what's up, man?" Dave said, turning to Bobby.

"Yo, man, I don't want some white dudes to be comin' in here givin' my kids no candy." Bobby's voice was beginning to take on the high pitch of someone upset.

Dave grabbed him by the arm, dragging him off a few feet. "Bobby, are you crazy? Those guys are connected!" whispered Dave with force.

"Made?" asked Bobby, with a sudden change of attitude. It was one thing to have connections with the Mafia, but it was altogether different to be a "made" member.

"Made," came the grim reply.

"Oops." Bobby had forgotten Dave was selling drugs for the Mafia.

This revelation would have sent most hustlers into appeasement mode. Bobby knew he had to handle the situation carefully but at the same time was determined not to show weakness. He walked over to the two white men. "Listen, I meant every word I said," Bobby told them earnestly. "But let me ask you somethin'. What would you do if you came home and some black guy was givin' your kid candy? You would have done the same thing I did. Tell me you wouldn't," he challenged with subdued voice.

The one Italian looked at him and smiled. "You know what, bro? You're right," he conceded.

Bobby continued. "Listen, I got no beef which you guys, but listen, that's my daughter. If I don't protect her, who will?"

"You know what?" said the Mafioso. "I like you." He was undoubtedly accustomed to people cowering in fear around him. They could respect someone who would stand up for his children—even to the Mafia.

Bobby had showed the coolheaded courage that had gotten him through many difficult situations in the past, but it didn't take long for the life of crime to take its toll on him once again. Before long, his emotional life deteriorated to the point that he was becoming rash and increasingly dangerous.

Goin' Mean

CHAPTER TWENTY-ONE

Going Mean

One afternoon, Bobby and Stevie were driving through Lakeview on Sunrise Highway when a white guy in a Toyota rashly cut right in front of Bobby's car, causing him to slam on his brakes to avoid a collision. Bobby slammed his hand on the horn, giving the man a long, loud rebuke. The guy's response was to stick his hand out of his window and flip the bird to the angry motorist behind him.

Oh man, groaned Stevie. He knew his brother too well to think this kind of provocation would go unanswered.

Moments later the Toyota was forced to a stop at a red light. Meanwhile, Bobby had calmly reached into the glove box and pulled out a hunting knife. Once he stopped his Cadillac, he walked up to the other man's car and slashed his face with the knife. He then calmly returned to the car, leaving the man bleeding and screaming.

Stevie was in shock at the utter calmness with which his brother had just acted. *Man*! he thought to himself. *He acts like he just stepped out to ask someone directions. Who is this man*?

Yes, Bobby Lloyd had changed over the years. There was something very dark about him now that even his brother couldn't understand.

****

On another occasion Bobby took Godfrey and Audrell, his "soldiers" since prison, and drove to Wyandanch, a predominantly black community on Long Island. Audrell needed some cigarettes, so Bobby pulled his big Caddie into the parking lot of a convenience store located in the neighborhood. Audrell entered the store, leaving Bobby and Godfrey chatting in the front seat.

Standing against the wall of the store was a tall, lean black guy of about thirty years. He had the hungry look of a doper, a look Bobby recognized well. The guy took stock of the Cadillac and then fixed his gaze on Bobby as he sat in the driver's seat with the window open. "Yo," said the drug addict. "You guys look like you got some money. I should just take it," he announced, voice full of bravado.

Bobby looked at him with utter disdain. "What?! Are you outta your mind?" Before the man had a chance to respond, Bobby turned to Godfrey. "Shoot him." A look of confusion came over Godfrey's face. He was an expert in karate and could easily pound this fool into the ground for insulting his boss. But shoot him, over that? On the other hand, this was Bobby Lloyd speaking and Godfrey had long since learned to do what he was told.

"Bobby, this punk's a piece a' dirt!" argued Godfrey. By now the stranger was getting nervous.

Bobby looked intensely at Godfrey. "I said SHOOT HIM!" The words came forth with such force and deliberateness that there was no mistaking the menace in them. Bobby well understood the authority he wielded on the streets. That authority was not lost on the doper, who scampered into the store, with a look of utter terror written across his face.

Now Bobby was laughing. Godfrey was relieved but still confused. "Bobby, did you really want me to shoot him?"

"I don't know," chuckled his boss. The whole episode was suddenly hilarious to him.

"Man, don't ever do that to me again!" Godfrey exclaimed.

****

By this point, Bobby was resolutely bent on restoring the operation that had made him so rich and powerful before entering prison. But his efforts were continually being thwarted. For one thing, most of the dealers he had supplied had either found other connections, gone to prison, or been killed. He was becoming increasingly frustrated over the situation.

One morning he and Godfrey were driving down Lakeview Boulevard when he spotted a junkie who owed $100 to Audrell. Bobby whipped the car to the curb. "Godfrey, get out and give that boy a beatin'," he commanded.

Godfrey understood that in the world of drugs, the pusherman could not afford to be viewed as soft. He pulled himself out of the passenger seat and approached the man. "Yo, where's our money?" he demanded, slapping the hapless junkie across the face.

Bobby had something else in mind. He got out of the Cadillac, shaking his head in disgust and beat the man to the ground. As he lay there in a fetal position on the sidewalk, Bobby kicked him in the stomach for good measure. "That's how you beat a man!" he roared to his associate.

Bobby's position as a mid-level pusher should have been above beating up a junkie for a hundred bucks. But he was losing control. Bobby Lloyd had always been able to set aside his natural compassion to fight someone when necessary, but now he was becoming the kind of animal who enjoyed hurting people.

****

About a year after he was paroled, a friend set up a meeting for Bobby with a Pakistani. "I will give you two pounds of pure cocaine if you will kill my partner," the man said, seemingly without any qualms.

Bobby considered the proposition for a moment. *Business hasn't been going so well, and I sure could use a couple of pounds of coke*, he said to himself. *Man, that must be worth almost a million.* "I'll do the job," he announced.

Over the next few minutes, the Pakistani gave him all the necessary details to accomplish the job. On a specified date, a limousine would be picking the partner up at their home and taking him to JFK Airport. Bobby could hit him on the way to the airport. "I need this man out of my life," said the man, handing the precious package to Bobby.

As Bobby and Godfrey planned the job, they could see that there was only one route to leave the house on the way to the airport. They picked a spot where Audrell would block the limo with a stolen car, Bobby would approach the car and shoot him, and then they would escape in the stolen vehicle. They would dump that car a couple of blocks away and drive off in another one.

On October 22, 1979, Bobby and Godfrey were positioned for the hit. But the limousine didn't show up. They waited half an hour before driving by the couple's house. It wasn't there either so they darted to JFK. There must have been a dozen limos at the terminal. Bobby ran inside, trying to find a flight to Pakistan. *Damn, why didn't I find out about the flight?* he fumed at himself. After an hour of futile searching, he gave up and went home.

He didn't have the Pakistani's phone number so he waited for the man to contact him. Several days went by and he didn't hear from him. Finally, Bobby approached the mutual contact, but he hadn't heard from him either. It concerned him that he had nearly a million dollars worth of this man's drugs and hadn't accomplished the job for which he had been paid. He never heard from the man again and had no idea whether or not the man's partner was eventually murdered.

What Bobby didn't understand was that the Holy Spirit was now zeroing in on his life. Dianne was bombarding heaven on behalf of Bobby and her family. She would not accept what most were saying, that he was a lost cause.

1st Wedding Anniversary
1980

CHAPTER TWENTY-TWO

A New Lifestyle

"Bobby, you gotta look up Dianne," said one of her sisters. "She's toting a Bible around, singing in a choir and constantly going to church. She's worse than she ever was on drugs."

Bobby immediately paid a visit to Dianne. "What are you *doing*?" he demanded, forgoing any formalities. "Your family is in an uproar. What's goin' on with you?"

"Well, why don't you come to church with me tonight and find out for yourself?" she retorted.

"Okay, I will," said Bobby, to her utter surprise. And that very evening Bobby Lloyd attended his first church service. The mixed couple pulled into the parking lot of the "Tabernacle" a few minutes late. As they walked up to the front door, Bobby was quick to note the shiny Cadillac gleaming in the pastor's parking spot. *That's just like mine.*

As they entered the spacious sanctuary, an usher—like a well-trained bellhop—was immediately available to guide them to a seat. The choir and congregation were already in full swing, with a definite black gospel flavor to their singing. To his surprise, Bobby enjoyed the music but, for the most part, he was drinking in the scenery around him more than the message of the songs.

People were well dressed: whites, blacks, and Hispanics all decked out in their respective finery. The ushers were especially impressive, wearing matching sport coats and slacks. Then he noticed the bulge under the left arm of one of them. He glanced at another usher who had the same protrusion. "Those dudes are strappin'," Bobby whispered to Dianne.

"You're crazy," she responded. But Bobby knew his business; these guys were packing guns.

After nearly an hour of music, the pastor finally got up to speak. *Alright, this is where everything goes downhill. He's gonna get up there and tell us we're all sinners headed for hell.* But to his surprise, the pastor's message was totally positive. Practically all he talked about was how the Lord wants to prosper His children.

"Every time you sow that seed in the offering, the powers of Heaven are loosed on your behalf!" he thundered. "You cannot, I said, you cannot out-give God!"

"Amen!" shouted an exuberant white man sitting nearby.

"Go on, pastor," added a black woman, "Go on and tell it like it is!"

Thirty minutes later, the pastor concluded his sermon with a prayer of blessing over the congregation. And then it was over. The brightening lights served as a cue for people to begin talking to one another. Others began moving quickly for the exits, but Bobby Lloyd remained planted in his seat, soaking it all in.

An earnest seeker of God might have had a difficult time accepting much of what had just been observed. But Bobby Lloyd was not an earnest seeker. The only reason he had even attended the service was to try to better understand what was going on with this young woman with whom he was strangely connected. The truth is that instead of provoking critical thoughts about the pastor's car, the bodyguard/ushers, and the prosperity message, the whole service had left a most favorable impression on him. *I could do this.*

And so it was that Bobby began attending church with Dianne. He hadn't bought into the whole Christianity thing like Dianne had, but he liked the pastor's lifestyle enough to go along with it all. But Bobby's main interest was in Dianne. Her style of religion, much to his relief, was not intolerable like he had expected it to be.

Over the coming weeks in the summer of 1979, Bobby and Dianne spent increasingly more time together. There were a number of things about her that made her stand out from all of the other women he'd had relationships with. For one thing, she was a member of the Jack family—that wild clan of white neighbors with whom he'd had a special connection since boyhood. She was also the only girl who had written or visited him while he was in the joint. All of his other women—and there had been hundreds over the years—were there for the good times but disappeared when his life unraveled.

After pondering these issues one day, Bobby finally announced to himself, *Dianne's just special. That's all there is to it. She's the only woman I know that I would want to spend the rest of my life with.*

Bobby and Dianne were married in the fall of 1979. But if Dianne had any illusions about a Godly marriage, the wedding should have set them to rest. The best man and the ten groomsmen were either drug dealers or users. Dianne, on the other hand, had one attendant, a maid of honor, her faithful friend and spiritual mentor, Christine. Although it may have seemed un-balanced to some, to Dianne it was an expression of the power of the God she so loved and served. Today, most, if not all, the groomsmen are either with the Lord or serving Him in some capacity!

Meanwhile, Bobby still had the issue of appeasing his parole officer (P.O.), and now Dianne too. Rather than going to work for someone else, he decided to start his own automotive shop:

Bodana (Bobby-Dianne) Motors, located on Lakeview Avenue, right down the street from Rockville Centre. To his P.O., his wife, and the neighborhood, Bodana was a legitimate business, but actually it was only a front for a heroin dealing operation. The mechanics who worked for him were junkies and his main clientele were dealers. It could get downright comical when unsuspecting people brought their cars in to be worked on. Sometimes they would come back to find the mechanic lying under their car nodded out. Then there was the time the guys put the wrong transmission in a man's car.

Dianne worked at a hair salon on Wednesdays so Bobby did his best to limit his illegal activities to that day. Every Wednesday morning, like clockwork, gangsters began showing up looking for product. It was the perfect setup because he could have unknown people arriving throughout the day without raising suspicions. A dealer would arrive for an oil change and leave with a bag tucked under his seat.

One Wednesday, about six weeks after they got married, the Holy Spirit impressed Dianne to stop by the shop for an unexpected visit. The first thing she noticed when she arrived was the array of "gangster leans" that only drug dealers would drive. Standing around were an assortment of gangsters and their women—girls sporting the unmistakable look of streetwalkers.

Bobby froze when he saw her walk in, looking around. But all Dianne said to him was, "I'll see *you* at home." He knew what that meant. When he came home that night, the two got into a terrible argument. "You either get out of the business or I'm leaving!" Dianne finally said.

"I can't get out of the business," countered Bobby. "This is what I do for a living!"

It was clear she could not force him to change, so she had a huge decision to make. After praying about it, Dianne decided that her marital covenant with Bobby was similar to her covenant with God. If she could break one she could break the other. She decided she would stay, in spite of his lifestyle.

It wasn't long, though, before Dianne realized that there was more to her husband's lifestyle than simply running a criminal enterprise, such as other women, which Bobby continued to see on a regular basis.

One day, Dianne received a phone call from one of his girlfriends. "Hey Dianne, I just thought you would want to know that I just got out of bed with Bobby," the mean-spirited girl said with a chuckle.

"Fine, if that's what you need to do, have sex with him in a bathroom stall or whatever, you go right ahead," Dianne retorted. "At the end of the day he comes home to me!"

Not only did Dianne get most nights with her husband, but she insisted that he spend Sundays with her as well. Most weekends all their children were also with them. The mothers of Bobby's five daughters were drug addicts, in and out of jail as Bobby was, so the girls liked being with Dianne. Paula, the oldest at age 16, was Ulamay's daughter. Dawn and Monique (ages 11 and 10) were Cheryl's, and Chante and Bobbette (6 and 5) were from Loretta. Dianne took the girls, along with her son Gregory (now 11), to church, children's church, youth events, plays, and circuses, whatever she could do. She insisted Bobby come to church and afterwards sit down to Sunday dinners with them. She was trying to bring some stability into the girls' very dysfunctional lives. And so once a week, in the midst of his life of drugs, sex, and crime, Bobby Lloyd faithfully attended church as a family man and spent a quiet afternoon with his wife and children.

****

One day Audrell called Bobby on the phone. "Bobby, I want you to come down to Brooklyn tonight. Blue Magic is performing at The Biz and I want to introduce you to them."

In the world of Rhythm and Blues, Ted Mills and Blue Magic were huge. They had formed in 1972 and within two years their hit singles *Sideshow* and *Three Ring Circus* sold millions of records and put them in elite status for R & B bands. Bobby was skeptical about Audrell's claims. *How could Audrell get in with those dudes? It don't make sense to me, but I've never known him to be a liar.*

Bobby knew Blue Magic was a class act, but he was unprepared for the pandemonium that was at the nightclub when he arrived. Cars were jammed into every spot available. Throngs of people were being turned away from the front door. A local news truck was parked in front. *Man, there ain't no way I'm gettin' in there. Where's Audrell?*

Bobby found a parking spot two blocks away and hurried to the club. He was relieved to see Audrell standing out front. "Yo, 'Drell. Are we gonna be able to get in?"

"You wit' me, Bobby," Audrell said, pointing at himself. "We own dis place tonight, blood!"

The two maneuvered through the crowd to the front door. The doorman saw Audrell and passed them through. Audrell slipped him some cash as they walked by to show his appreciation.

Bobby and Audrell had front row seats. What a show it was! Not only could these musicians sing, but they danced as well. Bobby thoroughly enjoyed the whole performance.

When they had finished the final number, the lights came on and people began heading for the door. "Come on, Bobby. Let's go to the back." With that, Audrell led his boss to a side door that opened into a narrow hallway going behind the stage. There were already a dozen girls clamoring to see the musicians, their path blocked by a huge bouncer.

Now we'll see if Audrell is just talkin' stuff. "Please take me in with you," one beauty cooed, as they walked by. To Bobby's amazement, the bodyguard clearly recognized Audrell. "How ya doin', 'Drell? Who you got whicha?"

"This is my man Bobby Lloyd."

"Alright Bobby, you're good. Go on through."

The pair proceeded into the back room. "Hey guys, I want you to meet Bobby Lloyd," Audrell said, like a school kid proudly presenting his daddy.

"So *this* is Bobby Lloyd," responded Ted Mills, checking out the gangster. "We finally meet him." It quickly became apparent that Audrell had told them all about him. The musicians immediately began asking Bobby all kinds of questions about his lifestyle.

"Do you carry a piece?"

"Have you ever shot anyone?"

"How'd you get your start?"

"How'd you make it to the big time?"

"Did you really know Nicky Barnes?"

Bobby did his best to satisfy their curiosity without incriminating himself in anything. After all, he didn't know these guys personally. After the excitement died down, Ted made his way over to where Bobby was standing. The two black men talked and clearly enjoyed each other's company. Eventually, the musicians headed to their hotel rooms and Bobby and his crew drove back out on the Island.

The next day Bobby received an unexpected call from Ted. "Bobby, I'm in Brooklyn. Can you pick me up?"

"Yeah, sure." Bobby hung out with Ted and his woman that day and brought them to his apartment that evening. Dianne was not happy that Bobby brought them there to spend the night. "They're not married," she said through gritted teeth to him in the hallway.

"Come on, Dianne. These are good people." In his unregenerate mind, a man spending the night with his woman was something wholesome. "It's not like he brought a hooker with him!"

Over the coming years, Ted and Bobby became very close friends. Ted felt like Bobby was one of the few people he could really trust and would often share with him his personal struggles.

"Bobby, I need you to hold onto something for me," Ted explained, handing his friend a thin package one day. "It's my platinum record. Can you keep it for me?"

"Sure, Ted." And for seven years it sat at Bobby's mother's house in Rockville Centre until Ted eventually picked it up, but for some reason he didn't take everything. He left some plaques. That was also the last time Bobby saw Ted Mills.

Wedding Festvities

Greg & Dawn
1979

Born Free
1985

CHAPTER TWENTY-THREE

Quitting the Business

By the early '80s, a definite change had come to New York street life. It was hard to pin down exactly what instigated that change. Crime had always been risky business, but there was a certain degree of order to it. The rules of the streets were certainly complicated, but they were in place and understood. However, somewhere along the line the unspoken rulebook governing street life had been neglected. Criminals and street people were doing things they were not supposed to be doing. People were snitching on each other as if it didn't matter. Drugs like PCP and crack cocaine were fueling even more deviant behavior. New gangs, like those from Colombia, were showing a level of viciousness not seen before. Street life was more dangerous and unpredictable than Bobby had ever seen it.

As if all of that wasn't bad enough, a rival black gang set up a new heroin-dealing ring in Bobby's area. Then, on top of everything else, a strange series of events happened. First, someone shot-gunned Solomon Glover to death in the Skyway Motel in Queens. (He had managed to get out of prison on parole.) Then, another dealer named Junior was shot by an unknown person as he was getting into his car. After that incident, a couple of other local dealers were killed. These could have been isolated incidents or they could have been the work of the new gang. No one knew for sure.

Bobby found himself constantly looking over his shoulder when he was out in public. He became especially apprehensive whenever he approached his car, not knowing if there was a bomb planted under it or if someone was lurking around ready to gun him down.

All of this began to take its toll on Bobby's mind. There were times he would even wake up in the middle of the night in a cold sweat. A few years back he had been utterly fearless, but now it seemed that fear was his constant companion.

Man, I need to get outta this business. Just the thought brought his mind back to the movie *Superfly*. The movie's plot revolved around Priest, the central figure, trying to get out of the business. *I never understood why he wanted out. Now I get it. He got tired of the constant stress involved with pushing drugs. I never thought about it before, but there's a lotta stress in this business. I gotta get out, but how do I do it? What would I do for a living?*

Bobby didn't realize that there were spiritual dynamics involved. The paranoia he was experiencing is something sinners have always faced.[14] But even beyond that spiritual law was the fact that he had a praying wife. At the little church in Balwin, Dianne sat weekly with powerful prayer warriors—sister Elaine Cedzich, Gail Jensen, and a handful of others—interceding nonstop for her husband, and the Holy Spirit was beginning to awaken Bobby's heart to the emptiness of life without God. Bobby found himself longing for a better life. He was still very much addicted to drugs, sex, and the prosperity his lifestyle afforded him, but, at the same time, he was also growing increasingly unwilling to pay the price to maintain these things.

To be sure, God was at work behind the scenes in Bobby's life. One more incident was about to happen that would push him over the edge. It all began with a minor dilemma he faced

---

14 *The wicked flee when no one is pursuing, but the righteous are bold as a lion* (Proverbs 28:1).

one Sunday afternoon. John, who had become his partner, had arranged a meeting to pick up some powder from a new source that evening. The problem was Dianne. Bobby had promised her that he wouldn't do business on the Lord's Day. He cringed at the thought of telling her.

"Honey, I'll catch up with you at church," Bobby said as nonchalantly as possible that afternoon. "I need to make a quick run."

Dianne had noticed he had his street clothes on, and she made a call to Christine, her spiritual mentor and maid of honor at their wedding, and asked her to pray. Encouraged, she then told her husband, "Bobby, you promised that Sundays are mine. There is no compromise on this issue." Her level of resolution surprised him. But this was a meeting he couldn't miss. The more he insisted on going, the louder was her response. It was clear she wasn't about to give in on this. In Dianne's mind, Sundays were the only thing they had together as a couple. If they couldn't commit to spending this one day together every week, there was no marriage.

Once he saw that she wasn't going to give in, he called his partner. "John, I'm not gonna be able to make it tonight. Take a couple of the guys with you."

Bobby and Dianne arrived home from church around midnight. The phone was ringing when they walked in the door. John's girlfriend was nearly hysterical. "Bobby, John got ambushed tonight. He got shot in the chest. Curt is dead."

"You gotta be kiddin' me," Bobby said, trying to absorb the information. About a month before, John had been telling him about this guy he had met who supposedly had some great connections for heroin. Bobby's interest had been piqued because a drug dealer can never have too many sources for dope. Finally, a deal was set up to buy some product. "Hey, if it's good stuff, we'll buy more," John had told the trafficker, agreeing to meet him in an industrial area of Queens. Unbeknownst to him, the whole thing had been a set-up.

It was a couple of days before Bobby could get in to visit John in the hospital. He had been shot in the right lung. It was a serious wound, but he would survive. "Bobby, we were set up!" John rasped, clearly struggling to get his words out. "Man, it's a good thing you didn't go. Curt was in the passenger seat and got shot in the head. It would have been you sitting there!"

"What happened?" Bobby asked. "Did you get there early to case the place like I said?" Bobby was never casual in his approach to drug deals like this. He had heard too many stories of guys who had been murdered and robbed because of carelessness.

"Well, it didn't work out for us to get there early," John said. "Sam was driving his Fleetwood, Curt was riding shotgun, and I was in the back. We were sitting out there in this big parking lot waiting for them to show up. One of the guys came out of the warehouse, but then he went right back in. We just sat there waitin' to see what they were gonna do. A few minutes later he comes back out with two other dudes. Curt started to get outta the car and those dudes opened fire on us. It was the Fourth of July out there, Bobby. We didn't have a chance!"

"What happened next?"

"Man, I don't know. I must a' passed out when I got shot. The next thing I know, I'm here at the hospital."

"Did Sam get shot?"

"Yeah, Felicia told me a bullet must a' grazed his head. He got knocked out, but he's okay. Those dudes must a' thought we was all dead."

"They took the money, right?"

"No, Bobby. That's the weird thing. They didn't even take the money."

"Wow. This must have been a hit. I'd put money on it that it was that new gang trying to take me out. Listen, you just take it easy. You need some rest. You need a lotta rest."

Bobby had a long talk with himself, driving home that day. There were two things that stood out very clearly to him. First, if Dianne wouldn't have given him such a hard time about going, he would be laying in the morgue right now. It was obvious that God had intervened to spare his life. The second thing was that he wanted out of the business. *How many snitches am I gonna have to kill to keep from going to jail? How many shootouts will I have to get in to stay alive? Am I really ready to go to war with these guys to keep my business? Does it mean that much to me? No, that's it. I'm done. I'm givin' the business to Audrell.*

(In 2010, Bobby had the opportunity to minister to Audrell. Shortly afterwards, Audrell died face down on the streets of Washington DC, shot in the back numerous times and left for dead.)

Christmas
1978

CHAPTER TWENTY-FOUR

Into the Kingdom

In the weeks following the ambush, events began to transpire that would greatly alter the direction of Bobby and Dianne's lives. First, Dianne's father was diagnosed with cancer. By the time it was discovered, it had worked its way through his whole body. Every day, Dianne spent long hours caring for her father. She also began to minister to him. He agreed that he needed to make his life right with God but insisted that he wouldn't say the "sinner's prayer" unless the Black Knight would say it with him.

At this time Dianne was attending a small Bible study in the basement of the Burns' family home. A young pastor, 19 years old, whom Dianne had met in "The Tabernacle" was pastoring the church. Pastor Mike accompanied Dianne to pray for her Dad. Of course, as was typical of the Black Knight, he was hours late, but they waited patiently singing songs and praying. In strutted Bobby, dressed to the hilt for the street, wide brimmed hat, western boots, tailored pants, and leather jacket. Mr. Jack reached for Bobby's hand and there in that hospital room the Black Knight said a prayer that would forever change his life. Mr. Jack died only days later. Bobby left once again to carry on his business out of state, leaving Dianne alone to bury the father she adored and to lead her dysfunctional family through the much dreaded ordeal.

Bobby was not intending on coming up for the funeral, but one phone call from his father changed that. With Bobby gone, Pop was going to have to escort Dianne into the funeral home. That was enough for Pop. He called his son and in no uncertain terms demanded his return. Bobby was on the next flight up to New York. You don't mess with Pop. Bobby had learned that early in life.

While all of this was going on, Dianne found out that she had an ectopic pregnancy. Rather than attaching itself to her uterus, the embryo became lodged within her fallopian tube, a situation that can easily cause death. But because she was so involved in her father's situation, she continued to resist the doctors' insistence that she come in for surgery. Within days of her father's funeral, her fallopian tube ruptured and she was rushed into surgery. She lost a lot of blood and at first her blood wasn't reproducing itself. Her life was hanging in the balance.

In typical fashion, Bobby was at a loss about it all. He felt badly for Dianne, but the thought of losing her certainly wasn't devastating to him. He had been around so much death that he had become hardened to it. He loved Dianne in his own self-centered way. She had always been special to him, but the truth was his marriage was beginning to take a toll on him and so was the street. One of them had to go!

It took weeks of recuperation before Dianne was completely out of danger. Being laid up gave her a good opportunity to consider her life. One thing she couldn't get away from was the fact that her church was having no effect on Bobby's life. In fact, if anything it only encouraged his hedonistic lifestyle.

As if on cue, her close friend and maid of honor at their wedding, Chris, began to tell her about the church she and her husband Juan had gotten involved in. It was obvious from the things she shared with Dianne that her pastor was a Godly man. "Why don't you bring Bobby to a service, Dianne?"

"I just don't know if he will come," Dianne said.

Chris told her the couple, Curt and Gail Jensen, who lead worship were awesome and that Curt was a Las Vegas entertainer at one time and his wife made homemade chocolate! Chris knew Bobby had a sweet tooth. "Do you think he'd go over to their house for dinner? Maybe if he knew someone there, he would be more open to going to church."

The two women conspired and made a date for the following Monday night. Bobby and Dianne would come over for dinner and Dianne would give Curt a "perm." They were certain that Curt, the former entertainer, and Bobby would hit it off. And that's exactly what happened. In fact, because the perm didn't take in Curt's hair, they had to return twice more during the following week.

Interestingly, it wasn't Curt's past life that got Bobby's attention, but this couple's current lifestyle. It was so obvious that they enjoyed a healthy relationship with each other and their kids. *I've never had a relationship like that with Dianne or my kids. I need what these people have.*

When they invited Bobby and Dianne to visit their church the following Friday night, Bobby agreed. Sheepgate Assembly of God was a tiny church compared to the "Tabernacle." So it was very obvious when this couple entered the small sanctuary that they were new. As soon as Pastor Joe Cedzich saw Bobby that night, he felt an inexplicable burden for him. "Son, come up here. I want to pray for you," he said from the pulpit. Bobby dutifully obeyed and walked up to the altar. Pastor Joe didn't know anything about this well-dressed black man, but he laid his hands on Bobby and prayed a powerful prayer over him. Toward the end of the prayer, he felt a word from the Lord well up inside him. "Bobby, God just showed me that one day He is going to use your testimony to bring many souls into His Kingdom."

Bobby was deeply impacted. He had never experienced such utter sincerity from a person in his entire life. He *knew* this was a genuine word from the Lord. That Friday evening service was his first encounter with real Christianity.

In the following weeks, Bobby and Dianne were in church "every time the doors were open." There is no question that the Holy Spirit was working in Bobby's life.

During this period of time, Pastor Mike, the young preacher who had led Bobby to the Lord at Mr. Jack's hospital bedside, invited Bobby to accompany him to a Bible study he was holding on Monday nights in Marshals Creek, a small town in Pennsylvania. Bobby felt honored to be asked. So on Mondays, four men: Bobby, Pastor Mike and his assistant John, and Christine's husband Juan would pile into Pastor Mike's 73 Blue Cadillac Coupe Deville and take the three hour hike to Pennsylvania. Over the George Washington Bridge up all the way on 81 just over the Delaware Water Gap on Route 209 sat a little Italian Restaurant owned by a lovely couple from Long Island who had a heart to reach the people in their town. Bobby offered to do the driving for these trips so Pastor Mike would be relaxed to share the message. It seemed very generous of Bobby, but he had an ulterior motive. On the way, he periodically took a detour through Harlem and stopped to see his cousin, or so he said. It would be some years later that Bobby would confess to Pastor Mike that the stops he made were a convenient way to pick up his much needed heroin without alerting Dianne.

By this point he had quit selling drugs but, unbeknownst to the pastor, he was still addicted to heroin. Nevertheless, Bobby and Dianne continued to become increasingly involved in Sheepgate Assembly. Over the following months, Bobby began spending a lot of time reading the Bible. The more he read it, the more fascinated he became with it.

This fact was not lost on Pastor Joe, who eventually invited Bobby to take over the Friday night Bible study. Bobby was thrilled with this opportunity and it quickly became obvious to everyone that he was a gifted speaker.

Meanwhile, the remaining funds left over from his drug dealing days had run out. Bobby found a job as a mechanic with a local bus company. One day Bobby found the boss's wallet that had three thousand dollars in it. Realizing it was his boss's, Bobby walked into the office and said, "Ey, Rich you dropped something." The look on his boss's face had no hidden expression. The first thing he did was to check his money to find not a bill missing. Whether it was because of Bobby not stealing the money, or his ability, or because the Lord gave him favor, it wasn't long before his boss began increasing his responsibility and giving him raises.

Several months after he began the job, his boss called him into his office. "Bobby," he began, "we're having problems with our buses over at our other yard. In fact, if we don't get our buses in better shape, we're going to lose the big contract we have with the school district there. You've done such a great job here. I would like to transfer you over to that yard to help them get their buses up to par. There's a nice raise in it for you. Are you interested?"

"Sure, boss. When do I start?"

The following Monday, Bobby began reporting for work at the other yard. The fleet at that facility had fallen into disrepair. But Bobby went right to work on those buses, bringing one after another up to proper standards.

One Wednesday morning, a fire broke out on one of the buses Bobby hadn't yet worked on. The children escaped without injury, but the local newspapers headlined the story. This put pressure on local politicians who, in turn, came down on the owners of the bus company. Bobby became the scapegoat and was immediately fired.

Man, Lord! Bobby whined. *I finally get a job and start livin' my life for You and this is the thanks I get?!* But his complaints didn't cause life to get easier. In fact, now it seemed as though everything went wrong for him. For several weeks he was completely frustrated.

And things were about to get worse.

One Saturday night, Pastor Joe had a terrible dream that Bobby was going to get shot in the head if he didn't change his life. "What needs to change in his life, Lord?" asked the pastor. "Ask him," was the only response. So the following morning Pastor Cedzich pulled Bobby aside.

"Bobby, the Lord woke me up last night and told me that your life needed to change. Is there something I need to know about?"

Bobby was not above coloring the truth or even lying to get out of a tough situation, but he just couldn't deceive his pastor. "Pastor Joe," he responded earnestly. "I've been addicted to heroin for years. I've tried to quit, but I just can't seem to get a handle on it. I don't know what to do."

"Bobby, we're going to walk you through this. In the meantime, I've got to take you out of teaching the Bible. It wouldn't be right for me to leave you in that position."

Bobby broke down in tears—the first time he had cried since he was a little boy. He was overwhelmed with the feeling that he had betrayed the trust of this man. Nevertheless, he wasn't willing to relinquish his position without some kind of fight. Those Friday nights were like an anchor to Christianity for him. "Pastor Joe, please don't take the Bible study from me. I promise I'll change."

"Bobby, I believe the Lord was giving you a taste of how He will use you in the future, if you'll do the right thing. For now, you can keep on ushering and helping out around the church."

Bobby had never felt so discouraged in his entire life. He was ready to "throw in the towel" on Christianity.

Lord, what am I gonna do?

Bobby at Teen Challenge

Teen Challenge 1984

1986

Teen Challenge Brookly

CHAPTER TWENTY-FIVE

Teen Challenge

"Honey, the Assemblies of God have a program for drug addiction called Teen Challenge," Dianne said earnestly as the family drove to church. "I think it's what you need."

"I'm almost 40 years old," retorted an irritated Bobby. "I ain't goin' to no teen program."

"Bobby, that's just the name. Most of the guys are in their twenties and thirties."

Bobby just grunted as he pulled his Cadillac into the church parking lot. A young evangelist was visiting that morning. In the middle of the sermon, he suddenly changed the direction of his message. "Folks, I have to tell you about something that happened to me last weekend. Some friends took me to a place they call God's Mountain. There were nearly 200 ex-drug addicts praising the Lord. If it wasn't for the music, one look at this bunch would send you running! It was one of the most beautiful things I've ever seen. The name of the ministry that runs it is Teen Challenge."

Bobby and Dianne looked at each other incredulously. "You and Pastor Joe told him to say that," Bobby whispered.

"Bobby, I swear we didn't!"

When that guy gets done preachin', I'm gonna get to the bottom of this.

After the service, Bobby stalked up to the young preacher. "Yo, I wanna ask you a question and you better tell me the truth." The young man was somewhat startled by Bobby's intensity. "Why'd you start talkin' 'bout Teen Challenge?"

"Uh, I don't know," stammered the evangelist. "I wasn't planning on mentioning it, but when I was preaching, I just felt like I was supposed to tell what happened."

It was obvious to Bobby that he was telling the truth. There was no way around it: God wanted him in that program.

The following Friday, in February of 1984, Pastor Joe drove Bobby into Brooklyn to the original Teen Challenge center started some twenty years before by David Wilkerson. The induction staff member showed Bobby the room he would be staying in. "Okay, I'll go out to the car and get my stuff," offered Bobby.

When he entered the house with his third arm-load of clothing, the staff member exclaimed, "Whoa, man. We ain't got room for all this stuff! You got to send most of this back."

Pastor Joe was left with the extra baggage as Bobby settled into his new home. A couple of hours later, Norman Miller, the director, stopped by his room. "You just came into the program, right?"

"Yeah," answered Bobby.

"How would you like to go to a Knicks' game tonight?"

"Sure." Bobby couldn't believe it.

"Okay. Be ready to go at 6:30." *Man, this is gonna be alright!*

The next day Mr. Miller dropped by his room again. "Bobby, I'm going to a local church tonight to show a film about Teen Challenge. I want you to come with me."

"Okay."

So his second night in the program Bobby found himself with the director again. As the church filled up with people, Mr. Miller and the pastor were having difficulty getting the projector to work. The people were clearly getting impatient. "Bobby," Miller said, "go up and share something for a few minutes."

"Okay." So Bobby went to the pulpit and began sharing his testimony. After 15 minutes he dropped all pretenses and just started preaching. The people in the church loved it. "Amen, brother, preach it!" one lady cried out.

"Come on, now!" added an elderly black lady.

Meanwhile, Mr. Miller got the projector working and started the film. Bobby walked to the back of the sanctuary beaming. His moment of glory was short-lived. "What did you think you were doing up there?" whispered the director. "I didn't tell you to go up there and preach!"

"What came over me, came over me," responded Bobby, somewhat defiantly. Norman Miller chuckled at the brashness of this upstart.

Typically the last thing a director would do is to pay special attention to a new student. It's a sure recipe for trouble. But Bobby Lloyd was not a typical drug addict coming off the streets. He had been a high-powered dealer, accustomed to making ten times the annual income this director earned. Norman Miller didn't understand any of this, but the Lord did. He knew how important it was for Bobby to get a solid start to this new life. And it worked. For the next several weeks, Bobby threw himself into the program, diligently doing everything asked of him.

Ten weeks after arriving, Mr. Miller called him into his office. "Bobby, we need to make room for a new student and we feel that you're ready to move on to the next phase of the program. You need to get your bags packed. You're heading for Lake Champion in Glen Spey." Within the hour, one of the staff members was driving the ex-gangster into upstate New York.

While Bobby was enjoying the leisurely ride into the country, Norman Miller called Mr. Rios, the director of the program at Lake Champion. "Jose, I'm sending up a guy named Bobby Lloyd to be your assistant," he said, chuckling.

"What do you mean?"

"Listen, when this guy started the program, I thought he was going to take my job! He ain't a bit bashful about telling you how to do your job. So, I figured now that he's got me trained, I would send him up there to train you!"

It's expected that First Phase students are going to be somewhat difficult. After all, many of them have been living in the streets for years. But by the time they get into Second Phase, they are expected to be more submissive to authority. Such wasn't to be the case for Bobby Lloyd, whose spiritual immaturity began to show.

It happened one evening when the guys were assembled for their 7 p.m. chapel service. The staff member who was supposed to lead worship was late and the other guys took the opportunity to cut up and become boisterous. Even though he still had rough edges, Bobby was serious about the program and didn't appreciate their flippant attitude. So when the staff member still had not shown up by 7:20, he decided he would lead worship himself.

The next morning Bobby was summoned to the director's office.

"Pack your bags, Bobby. You're leaving," said Mr. Rios grimly.

"Whadya mean?"

"We're throwing you outta the program."

"For what?"

"Because you took over the prayer meeting last night."

"The guys were foolin' around and stuff," Bobby countered. "I was just tryin' to help out."

"It doesn't matter," came the cold reply. "It wasn't your place to do that."

"You know what? Fine! It ain't no sweat off my back." Bobby was angry at what he felt was a complete overreaction to what he had done. He started walking toward the door, full of defiance. But just as he reached for the door handle, a tremendous sense of sorrow overwhelmed him. He felt like he was about to lose something very valuable. In one instant, he went from angry rebellion to tears. "I'm sorry, guys," he blubbered. "This is all new to me."

He went up to his room and started packing his belongings. A few minutes later his counselor arrived. "Bobby, put your things away. You don't have to leave. Listen, what you did in the chapel last night was all pride, and we cannot allow our students to operate in pride here. But when we saw you crying in Mr. Rios's office, we knew that your heart has been pierced by the Lord. You need to learn some things, but now we know that you really are sincere."

Yes, Bobby was a sincere baby Christian, but he was a man of enormous pride and it wasn't going to go away quickly. By this point in his life, Bobby Lloyd's reputation as a fierce fighter, a feared gangster, an affluent drug pusher, a ladies' man, and a "stand-up" guy with a great personality was widespread. He took enormous pride in the cars he drove, the clothes he wore, and the women he showcased. He loved the fact that aspiring gangsters would do their utmost to impress him, that beautiful girls openly showed their desire for him, and that he was highly respected in various black communities of Long Island. For the past twenty years he had been viewed as a larger-than-life figure throughout much of the Long Island metropolitan area.

Christianity was now asking Bobby Lloyd to walk away from the persona that had lavished him with man's adoration. The following excerpt from a book on overcoming pride provides insight into the magnitude of the challenge Bobby faced as a new believer:

Unquestionably, pride is one of the most prominent subjects addressed in Scripture. The Bible uses at least 17 different words (and countless derivatives) to describe this spiritual disease. However, no matter which term is used, there is almost always a connotation of height: something high, rising, exalted, or being lifted up. Thus, a proud person has a high estimation of himself and lifts himself above those around him. This concept of self-exaltation forms the basis for our working definition of pride: *Having an exaggerated sense of one's own importance and a selfish preoccupation with one's own rights.* It is the attitude that says, "I am more important than you and, if need be, I will promote my cause and protect my rights at your expense."

Pride is the governing principle of hell and the unredeemed world it influences. ... How utterly different is God's kingdom! His realm is governed by the innocent Lamb who allowed Himself to be slaughtered *for the sake of others.* He is "meek and lowly in heart." (Matthew 11:29 KJV) The presiding mentality of those who faithfully follow Him is low-mindedness. Such individuals prefer the needs and wishes of others above their own.

It takes awhile for the new child of God to get used to this selfless thinking. As he attempts to live by the governing principles of the kingdom of heaven, he soon realizes that his old, selfish ways of thinking are still very much alive within him. Indeed, he still has a flesh nature that is permeated by pride. He finds himself torn between the self-promoting mentality of this world and the self-sacrificing values of God's kingdom. [15]

This was the overwhelming issue Bobby faced as a new believer. The Holy Spirit had to completely remake him as a man. This process began in Teen Challenge where, for the first time in his life, he willingly subjected himself to the authority of other people. He was still high-minded, but at least his value system was dramatically altered. Humbling himself to others didn't come easily, but he could now see the importance of it. By the time he completed the program in December, 1984, Bobby Lloyd had the solid beginnings of a new life in Christ.

Pastor Joe with Bobby, alumni of the year

15 Steve Gallagher, *Irresistible to God,* Pure Life Ministries, Dry Ridge, KY, 2003, p. 19, 21-22.

Early days of Teen Challenge and Freedom Chapel

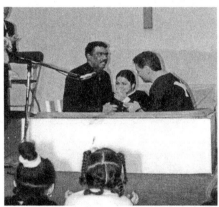

Bobby with "Youth at Risk"

CHAPTER TWENTY-SIX

Free Indeed!

Bobby returned home from Teen Challenge a changed man in many ways. He had new perspectives, new values, and new dreams. Unfortunately, much of the old still clung to him, like a bad smell that won't go away. For one thing, he couldn't escape the fact that he had hurt a lot of people over the years. Some were dead, others carried the scars of their encounters with Bobby Lloyd, still others lived in dread at the prospect of running into him unexpectedly.

Kenny was one such person. The last time he had seen him was when he received a terrifying pistol-whipping in Bobby's car. One day while stopped at a traffic light in Lakeview, Bobby casually glanced to his right and saw Kenny standing at the corner. *Oh man, it's Kenny!* Bobby immediately pulled his car to the curb and opened the passenger window.

"Kenny!" Bobby cried out, genuinely happy to see the guy.

Kenny squinted into the sun to see who it was. A look of terror came across his face when he realized it was Bobby. He immediately took off running. Bobby whipped his car around the corner and pulled alongside him. "Kenny! Hold it! Don't run! I'm not the same guy anymore."

Kenny slowed his pace maintaining a wary distance. "I know you," he said, eyeing Bobby suspiciously. "You ain't changed."

"Kenny, I love the Lord Jesus Christ, man," said Bobby earnestly.

Kenny stopped in his tracks. His shoulders slumped and he started crying. "Bobby, I got saved, too."

Kenny got in the car. "Kenny, I'm so sorry for the way I hurt you that day," said Bobby. "Please forgive me."

"Oh, man, Bobby," Kenny responded. "I had it comin'. I'm just glad we can put it behind us." The two talked about what had happened in their lives over the years. After a while, Kenny said with a mischievous look on his face, "But Bobby, I just gotta axe you one question."

"Sure, go ahead."

"What's up with this ride?" he asked, chuckling.

When Bobby was in his heyday, he always had a nice Cadillac. He was now driving a green, beat-up '71 Plymouth. The front left fender had been crunched at some point and the owner had done an amateurish job of plastering it with bondo.

"Well, while I was in Teen Challenge," Bobby told him sheepishly, "my wife decided I was too prideful so she sold my Cadillac and had this beater waitin' for me when I got out."

The two ex-criminals had a good laugh and were able to fellowship as brothers in the Lord that day. Not only was it a great relief to Kenny, but it was also healing to Bobby. While Kenny had carried around a load of fear all these years, Bobby had to face the reality of the damage he had done to so many people while he was a criminal. *At least that's one person I've hurt that I was able to make it up to.*

Meanwhile, Bobby had to get a job and become re-acclimated to normal life. He was hired back at the place where he was fired. The manger of the company said, "Bobby you were a sacrificial lamb." Later Bobby quit and got hired as a mechanic at Westbury Jeep dealership, a job he held for nine years. It was Bobby's new lease on life through the Lord that got him that job. At the end of the interview with Mike, the service manager, Bobby told Mike he was on life parole. Mike turned to Bobby and said, "I will call you." Bobby knew what that meant. Just as Bobby stepped up his pace to leave, Mike called out, "How soon can you start?" It was truthfulness in the Lord that got Bobby the job.

While he was at Teen Challenge, Dianne had continued to attend services at Sheepgate Assembly with all their children. Not long after Bobby returned, Pastor Joe asked to speak to the two of them.

"Bobby, Dianne," he said quietly, "I want to ask you to pray about something. We have a number of young people coming to church here and they just don't have any leadership. Would you guys pray about leading up our youth group?"

"Yeah," Bobby responded excitedly. "We sure will." Within days they let the pastor know they were happy to help out.

Bobby and Dianne threw themselves into this group of kids, which included their own four teenagers, Paula, Dawn, Monique, and Greg. The young people were so excited about the way things were going that they began bringing their friends to church. Before long, the youth group doubled in size. By the end of their first year, this church of 250 people had a thriving youth group of 50 dedicated young people.

Bobby and Dianne tried all sorts of different strategies to attract kids. They established a "youth night" every Saturday in which they would play games, watch Christian movies, or even hold Christian rock concerts. The young people passed out flyers to friends and other kids at school. Five hundred young people would attend some services. For four years Bobby quietly worked as a mechanic in the daytime and gave himself to those kids during the evenings. He began taking Berean Bible Courses through the Assemblies of God, an at home study. Soon his thirst for the Word of God led him to Christ for the Nations Bible Institute in Setauket. So, added to his already packed schedule, was Bible courses twice a week right after work, sometimes returning home by midnight.

****

One day, one of Dianne's brothers called Bobby and told him that Ricky—the brother-in-law whom Bobby had tried to kill with a knife—was dying of AIDS. "Bobby, we need to go see him before he dies," Dianne said.

"I ain't goin' to see him," Bobby answered. He was still bitter about being ripped off by someone whom he had helped

"You can't harbor that in your heart," she retorted. "You gotta let that go."

Bobby thought about it for a few minutes, before he finally agreed. "Yeah, I guess you're right. Okay, I'll go."

So they picked up two of her brothers and went over to Ricky's apartment. Ricky was a mere skeleton by now, weighing no more than 90 pounds. When Dianne's brothers walked through the front door, he smiled broadly at them. He appreciated them coming to visit him. Then Bobby walked in. As soon as he saw him, Ricky curled up on the couch in a fetal position and began trembling. "Please don't hurt me, Bobby," he whimpered.

"Ricky, I'm not gonna hurt you. I'm not the same guy anymore." Bobby hugged him and Ricky began to cry. Bobby just held him for a few minutes praying for him. Ricky died two weeks later.

****

Right before Bobby graduated from Teen Challenge, Dianne's youngest brother, Jimmy, entered Teen Challenge himself. Several years of drug addiction had left him hollowed out and desperate. Dianne was able to convince him to go into the program.

"Jimmy," she told him. "Look at how the Lord has changed Bobby. He can do that for you too!"

At the time, Jimmy blew her off. But a few days later, his life began crumbling around him and he finally agreed to go.

"Dianne and Miriam, my future wife, brought me to Brooklyn Teen Challenge at 1 a.m.," Jimmy later recalled. "At that point in time, I was anything but a willing candidate. The rage over my hopelessness was now focused at everyone who was trying to help. I was swinging, cursing, and resisting everyone. But the guys prayed for me. Finally, I slipped into a restless sleep..." [16]

It was a rocky beginning, but the next morning Jimmy gave his heart to God and never looked back. Nine months later he graduated the program. He married Miriam and the two of them stayed on as staff members. Eventually, Jimmy attended Central Bible College, an Assembly of God school in Springfield, Missouri. He returned to Long Island in 1989 with a commission from the Assemblies of God to begin a new Teen Challenge center.

The first person he thought of to assist him in this new work was his brother-in-law. "Bobby, do you want to help me pioneer this outreach?" he asked. "I need your help."

"Sure, I'm with you!" said Bobby.

"You know Bobby, you're thirteen years older than me and I've always looked up to you as a hero. But if we're going to work together, you have to let me be the leader."

Bobby knew he was right. "Absolutely, Jimmy. I'm here to help you in any way I can." The Lord would often remind him through the years of the Scripture so eloquently spoken by John

---

16 Jimmy Jack, *I Can Dream Again*, Freedom Publishing, New York, 2007, p. 86.

the Baptist of his cousin Jesus Christ." I must decrease so He may increase."

The fact is that for a couple of years Bobby had already been acting as a representative for Brooklyn Teen Challenge. When Long Island pastors encountered a young person desiring freedom from drug addiction, they would call Bobby to help facilitate the process of getting the guy or girl into the program. So it was only natural that he would be a co-founder of this new center on Long Island.

Jimmy and Bobby immediately began spreading the word about what they were doing. One of the first things they did was to hold street rallies in some of the worst neighborhoods of Long Island. They would set up huge amplifiers and speakers, play live music, and then preach to those who gathered. One of the first outreaches they held was in their old neighborhood in Rockville Centre.

Jimmy asked Bobby to share his testimony in that service. Bobby Lloyd was both feared and respected by the black community of Rockville Centre. He was known for being an extremely private person. He could shuck-and-jive with the best of them, but it was not in his nature to talk about personal issues. People crowded around, anxious to hear what he would say. Rather than talking about his life of crime and sin—a story they already knew—he felt the need to repent to them.

"Folks, I don't need to tell you how much I did to harm this neighborhood and what a terrible influence I was on the young people here," he said, tears streaming down his cheeks. "All I can do is acknowledge how wrong I have been. Will you please forgive me?" The people were shocked and quick to extend their forgiveness. It was another example of how much Bobby had changed inside.

Yes life had changed for the Lloyds and they began to desire a child of their own. Two Ectopic pregnancies and the surgeries that followed rendered Dianne unable to conceive naturally. After a short stint at an in-vitro fertility clinic at Yale University, the Lloyds quickly decided that would not be in their best interest. They began looking into adoption and were immediately discouraged from that also. American adoption process left a lot to be desired and was very unpredictable.

Much to their amazement, Dianne's niece Tina became pregnant and claimed the child would be bi-racial. This peaked their interest and they began the process with Tina to adopt this child. This too ended up a dead end, as Tina was erratic and indecisive and began to play games with them, manipulating them for money to the point of extortion. The handwriting was on the wall. This was going to end in disaster. Tina gave birth in March of 1986 to a beautiful bi-racial boy named Daniel and kept him.

Later that year in October, Paula, Bobby's oldest daughter, gave birth to her second child, a beautiful little boy. He was born crack addicted but otherwise healthy. Well, there was finally a boy in the Lloyd family. After 5 girls, Bobby was elated! By April of the following year, after much prompting from her parents, Paula entered New Life for Girls in the Bronx. At one o'clock in the morning, the day before she left, she dropped Robert, now 6 months old, off to the Lloyds for safekeeping. After several stints in different programs, Paula returned to the pipe, and it became apparent she was unable to take care of Robert. The Lloyds adopted Robert and finally Bobby had a son to call his own! Yes, Bobby Lloyd had truly changed. He was becoming a real family man.

One significant person who noticed the change in Bobby's life was his parole officer. Because he had been sentenced under the Rockefeller Act, Bobby was required to spend the rest of his life on parole. He had to stay in constant communication with his parole officer. Down through the years, his P.O. had seen other ex-felons seemingly change, only to revert back to their old lifestyles. He knew Bobby could end up being one more "flash in the pan," but the more he checked into his life, the more impressed he was.

On the morning of the Fourth of July, 1991—two years after Bobby and Jimmy birthed Long Island Teen Challenge—he decided to pay Bobby a visit. As Bobby approached the front door, he could see through the window that it was his parole officer standing there. Panic seized his mind. *My P.O. here on a holiday can only mean that he is violating me. What could this be all about?*

He opened the door and invited him in. "Bobby, I just want you to know that I've been watching your life very closely the last couple years," his P.O. began. "I have never seen a parolee do so much good as you have done through this Teen Challenge program. I finally got to the point that I told my boss that it is just wrong to keep you on parole. So we sent a special petition to Governor Cuomo seeking to release you from parole. He signed off on it this week. Here is your pardon," he said, handing Bobby the certificate. The ex-con was speechless.

Over the next three years, Bobby continued to do whatever he could to help out Jimmy with Teen Challenge. It was one more stepping stone toward his life's calling.

John 8:36 *If the Son therefore shall make you free, ye shall be free indeed.*

Jimmy & Miriam   1978

The Jack boys
1989

Bobby with David Wilkerson

1984   2008

George & Mary Cote

CHAPTER TWENTY-SEVEN

Clean Hands and Pure Heart

Bobby Lloyd was a changed man. There was no denying that. But there was one area of his life that remained unconquered: sex. He had been a sex addict since his teen years. Although he hadn't been unfaithful to Dianne since coming to the Lord, he still had a secret, tenacious addiction to pornography. It all came to a head one day in late 1985 in an unexpected, and rather amusing, way.

Bobby was walking along the seashore in the city of Long Beach thinking about some of the hurdles facing Teen Challenge. But no matter how much he tried to focus on the issues at hand, a persistent thought harassed his mind: *That luncheonette on the corner has the latest Penthouse magazine in it.* Every time the thought surfaced, he would attempt to squash it. *I'm not gonna look at that stuff again!* Back and forth the mental battle raged. Eventually, like so many times before, he gave in to what he thought was the inevitable defeat.

He entered the store and casually moved toward the magazine rack. Glancing around to make sure there was no one there who knew him, he grabbed the magazine and headed to the counter. As Bobby paid the cashier, the man slipped the glossy publication into a brown paper bag.

He turned around ready to make a beeline out the door, but standing directly in his path was one of the women who attended Sheepgate Assembly. "Hi, Brother Bobby," she gushed. "What an unexpected pleasure to run into you down here! I just want you to know how blessed I am by your life. Your testimony has been so powerful for the young people in our church." On and on she went.

Beads of sweat were popping out on Bobby's forehead. He unconsciously moved the bag and its offensive material behind him, his sweaty hands gripping it so tightly the bag began to tear. A feeling of nausea crept up his throat. Still the woman talked. After about five minutes of this one-sided conversation, she said, "Brother Bobby, you don't look very well. Maybe you should go home and get some rest."

"Yeah, I think you're right," Bobby agreed, bolting past her out the door. As he made his way down a side street, he noticed a storm drain. He tore the magazine up and threw it in. "That's it!" he yelled. "I will never look at this garbage again!"

God used this unlikely experience to break the bondage of pornography addiction in Bobby's life. He never looked at pornography again!

****

Eight years later, Helen Adams faced a dilemma. She and her husband were pastoring a large congregation on Long Island, but she also had a great burden about the moral deterioration occurring in her community. Every time she would see girlie magazines in a convenience store, or drive by a massage parlor, or notice an adult bookstore, she became upset. That righteous indignation compelled her to begin an organization—Suffolk Coalition Against Pornography (S-CAP)—which sounded far more impressive than its fledgling membership warranted. Nevertheless, the small group did their best to combat the inroads the sex industry had made in Suffolk County. But now, after two years, she was realizing that she could no longer assist her husband pastoring a church *and* head up this battle. The group needed someone who could devote himself fulltime to this war.

Unbeknownst to her at this time, two other couples from two other churches were also praying about the infiltration of the porn industry on Long Island and contacted the National Coalition Against Pornography (NCAP) in Cincinnati. Dr. Jerry Kirk, founder and president of Citizens for Community Values (CCV)[17] of Cincinnati, quickly connected the six interested persons and their churches. Helen organized a series of strategy meetings to consider how to move forward. NCAP sent Paul Mauer, and a steering committee was formed, Helen Adams, from First Baptist Church of Patchogue, George Cote, Hempstead Assembly of God, Frank Lafaro, Smithtown Gospel Tabernacle. As a representative of Teen Challenge, Bobby was invited to participate with other concerned citizens.

One of their primary goals was to find and appoint a new executive director. A handful of those present agreed to meet again to discuss the need more directly. "Take the next week to develop a list of potential people," Helen told the other leaders. "Maybe the right person's name will surface."

The group met to discuss the situation the following week. Although a number of the people didn't know him personally, Bobby Lloyd's was the only name on every person's list. Helen Adams called him right away. "Brother Bobby, a number of us have gotten together to find a director for S-CAP," she told him over the phone. "Your name came up repeatedly. Do you think you would be interested in being interviewed for this position?"

"Hmm, let me talk to my wife, Helen," he responded. "I'll get back to you."

---

17 Phil Burress later became the president of CCV.

"Absolutely not!" barked Dianne, when Bobby approached her with the idea. "There is no way you're getting involved with pornography—even if it is to fight it."

You know what? Bobby thought to himself. *Dianne's right. I hate the way porn is affecting our community, but I just can't get involved in this. Besides, I just got promoted to Service Manager at the Jeep dealership. Things are finally lookin' good for us. Why give all that up?*

But even after he told Helen he wasn't interested, the growing burden over the problem remained in his heart.

George Cote from Hempstead Assembly of God who knew Bobby through Teen Challenge called periodically to say he believed Bobby was the man for the job.

After a few months of prayerfully considering the position, Dianne unexpectedly said, "Honey, I've been praying about that position with S-CAP. You know, it just doesn't look like anything is going to open up fulltime with Teen Challenge. Maybe you *should* consider it."

Bobby knew what he needed to do. *I need to talk to Don Wilkerson.*

Don Wilkerson had helped his brother David begin Teen Challenge in the early '60s. He had years of experience dealing with drug addicts. When Bobby had graduated from Teen Challenge, Don took him under his wing and began to mentor him. He had also spent many hours over the years providing marital counseling for the Lloyds.

Bobby told him about the opportunity. "Bobby," Don said, "if this is of God, the thought will persist. If it's not of the Lord, it will dissipate. I'm going to be praying that the Lord will make it clear for you one way or the other."

Over the coming months, Bobby could not escape the sense of grief over what pornography was doing to ruin the lives of men, women, and children in his community. One morning he woke up with the conviction that he was supposed to take the job. He called Helen and George with the news right away.

So ten years after entering Teen Challenge, Bobby Lloyd was hired to head this organization. His first priority was to learn all he could about the battle over pornography. He read everything he could get his hands on—not just the Christian perspective but also what its proponents were saying. He also spent a lot of time with Helen, reviewing the organization's past accomplishments and setbacks and finding out about sponsors, volunteers, and local politicians who might be friendly to their cause.

Jerry Kirk flew him to Cincinnati, showing him how to structure a porn-fighting organization. When he returned, Bobby and the other board members decided to align themselves with CCV, changing the name to Long Island Citizens for Community Values (LICCV). George Cote would become the chairman of the Board and serve in that capacity for twelve years. During those years, he was instrumental, along with Paul Mauer and Jerry Kirk, in grooming Bobby into the Executive Director of one of the most highly acclaimed para-church organizations on Long Island

During their first meeting, they decided to begin the new endeavor by hosting a banquet. Six hundred women attended the special dinner and pledged $100,000 to launch LICCV.

Everything went well for the first couple of months, and Bobby resigned the position he had held at the Jeep dealership for nine years. But no sooner did he do so, then the economy crashed, causing those that pledged support to be unable to keep their commitments, leaving Bobby alone in an upscale office with little or no support and no money to continue to pay a secretary. It was time to regroup.

These weren't the only problems Bobby faced. Of much more concern was the LICCV board. It didn't take him long to realize that several of the directors of the founding board felt he was inexperienced and would not allow him to use his expertise in the culture of Long Island he had developed through representing Teen Challenge to steer this new found coalition. They were controlling and argumentative; Bobby was defensive and overly sensitive.

During one early meeting, one of the directors, who happened to be a school teacher, lectured him for twenty minutes about the importance of proper spelling in the letters he wrote. That was the final straw. Bobby blew up. "Listen, if I hear another word about my spellin' or my mistakes, I'm walkin' outta here. Y'all can do this thing yourselves!"

Bobby knew he was in the wrong spirit, but he also knew he needed board members who were supportive of his efforts. It was hard enough battling with the forces of darkness at work in the local culture without having to fight with his own board members as well.

As the funding for LICCV began drying up, Bobby found himself having to dip into his savings account time and time again to keep it afloat and pay his own bills. Even that money was soon gone, causing he and Dianne to miss a number of mortgage payments. If it hadn't been for Dianne's hairdressing business, they would have lost everything.

It was during this time that Dianne went into the office to answer phones for Bobby on her days off. Bobby and Dianne began to work diligently on new ideas; researching, training, and giving seminars on the workings of a Non-profit, traveling to Albany, Cincinnati, and Washington DC for development.

They gathered together a Volunteer Force, and Bobby tirelessly beat the pavement meeting with pastors, businessmen, political leaders, and law enforcement, sharing his vision for a safer Long Island. One business leader who wishes to remain anonymous was instrumental in recouping a majority of the funds that were committed to LICCV in the early days, allowing the Lloyds to continue this crucial battle. In addition, George Cote and Jerry Kirk stuck by Bobby, cheering him on and lending their professional talents wherever and whenever they could.

But God was behind it all, allowing them to learn—as so many others have throughout Church history—to trust Him even when everything seems lost. They both struggled on in the face of overwhelming discouragement. Little by little funds came in—always just enough to keep them from going under.

Many times during those first few years, Bobby was tempted to resign or even to disband the organization. But each time he felt like he was at the end of his rope, the Lord would send along an encouraging word or a needed donation.

One of those instances was a chance meeting at a Messianic Passover Meal. The Lloyds were invited by a long time friend and Messianic Rabbi, Ron Corbett. Bobby was strategically placed across from an Executive type woman who looked a little out of place at this religious function. Bobby quickly began to share his ministry, and before long it became apparent that this woman had a heart for the issue he was so passionate about: protecting women, children, and families from the harms of pornography on Long Island.

At the end of the evening, Ellen Cooperperson handed Bobby a card and offered him her expertise in the field of corporate consulting with her firm, Cooperperson Consultant Performance in Hauppague. For the next year Ellen and her staff poured into Bobby's professional life, empowering and equipping him to move LICCV to the next level and relevancy in the corporate culture. For the first time in his life, Bobby Lloyd was learning what it meant to trust someone other than himself—what it meant to trust the Lord.

During this time, the Lloyds moved to Suffolk County to accommodate the ministry that was now housed there in Huntington, over an hour away from Long Beach. It had begun to be a hardship to travel that far. All the children were now grown and settled in their own lives, some married with children, some working on careers. Bobby and Dianne bought a lovely home and lived there with Robert, now age five, who began to attend a private Christian School in Smithtown. One evening during an outreach, Bobby and Jimmy, Dianne's brother, called her into the Outreach Office and asked if she would pray about taking Daniel, her niece Tina's son, for six months until Tina finished the program.

Dianne was hesitant. Robert, who had just been diagnosed with ADHD, was a handful, and they had already gone a few rounds with Tina before Daniel was born. But after much prayer and consideration, the Lloyds of course said yes.

Daniel, much to their delight, was a very compliant and obedient, young boy, conscientious and full of joy. He was just what the family needed. What began as a few months quickly turned into years. The Lloyds received permanent custody of him and changed his name to Lloyd. Their quiver was full. Eight children. At events, "His, hers, ours and everyone else's" was the statement often quoted of their large family of very colorful children, having five different mothers and four different fathers, all different ethnicities. But they were one in every sense of the word.

Psalm 24:3-4 *Who may ascend into the hill of the LORD? Or who may stand in His holy place? He who has clean hands and a pure heart,*

Robert & Daniel

Christmas 1997

...ography Destroys!

...and Citizens For Community Values

STOP

Bobby & Dianne
"Walk for Decency"

Child Safety
Puppetry

...ESTROYS
FAMILIES

PORNOGRAPHY

PORN

Home Depot, 2004

CHAPTER TWENTY-EIGHT

Safe Streets to Dwell In

New York's Times Square district had been a gathering spot of theaters, burlesque halls, and honky-tonks since the 1870's. By the end of the Roaring Twenties, Broadway (and off-Broadway) musicals and plays had established Times Square as the leading entertainment area of the world. Over the following years, movie houses sprang up in the area, adding the latest Hollywood cinemas to the mix.

It wasn't long before the sex-for-sale industry moved into this budding tourist trap. As early as 1901, vice officers had identified 132 brothels operating in the area. [18] But as the district grew in prominence, city officials banished them from the immediate vicinity. For the first half of the 20th Century, sexual vice was kept to occasional streetwalkers plying their trade along side streets.

A subtle change began in the 1950's when edgy newsstands and bookstores began offering soft-core pornography and erotic literature. But it wasn't until 1966 that the incident occurred which changed the face of West 42nd Street for decades to come. A vending machine distributor named Martin Hodas outfitted thirteen movie machines with stag films and leased them to a number of bookstores. [19]

The popularity of these "peep booths" quickly caught the attention of the Mafia, who began buying up the assorted delis, camera shops, and pinball arcades that flourished along 42nd

18 James Traub, *The Devil's Playground,* Random House Publishers, New
    York, 2004, p. 30.
19 *Ibid.,* p. 119.

Street between Seventh and Eighth Avenues. These were gradually replaced with adult bookstores, massage parlors, and strip clubs.

By the mid-1970's, as Bobby Lloyd plied his trade some 75 blocks uptown in Harlem, West 42nd Street had become one mass of perversion. Vice officers had long since given up any attempt to curb the blatant sexuality being proffered along the strip. Magazines and film loops offered S & M, bestiality, and even child porn. Adult movie theaters blatantly exhibited XXX-rated pictures in their window displays on the street. One adult bookstore even had a TV set positioned in its window so passersby could watch clips of erotic movies right on the sidewalk. In 1981, *Rolling Stone* magazine rightly labeled it "the sleaziest block in America." [20]

To say that commercial sex had become entrenched in the area would be a vast understatement. Perversion had become the very soul of 42nd Street. The district that had once been the pride of New York had become a run-down eyesore. Officials lamented the loss of real estate value.

Mayor Ed Koch was the first politician to attempt to revitalize the area, but political infighting and internal bickering among those involved hampered his efforts. Mayor David Dinkins, Koch's successor, continued to champion the cause and, on the final day of his administration, signed a non-binding agreement with the Disney Corporation to rebuild the New Amsterdam Theater on 42nd Street.

Their efforts (and those of local citizens) paved the way for Rudy Giuliani, who stepped into the mayor's office in January 1994. His law and order platform had won him the job, and he saw the revitalization of the Times Square district as the crowning achievement of what he envisioned for his term in office.

---

20 As quoted by Lynne B. Sagalyn, *Times Square Roulette,* MIT Press, Cambridge, MA, 2001, p. 7.

Mayor Giuliani knew that the only way Times Square could attract legitimate businesses would be if his administration could somehow root out the sleaze shops that dominated the area. At this point there were 177 adult entertainment businesses in New York City (up from 131 ten years before), with 57 of them huddled in the Times Square area alone. It would take a monumental effort to purge the neighborhood of all of these businesses.

Unfortunately, prosecutors around the country had long since discovered that existing obscenity laws were ineffective in closing down adult businesses. An exaggerated perspective of the First Amendment stifled every attempt to jail those involved with proffering erotic material. The mayor needed a new tactic but didn't know what it was.

Someone mentioned the success that Jerry Kirk had had in cleaning up Cincinnati. One of Giuliani's aides called Kirk to find out if he could help. He sent Paul Maier, his right hand man, to New York. Paul would team up with LICCV's Bobby Lloyd to offer assistance.

The two men met with the mayor and the city council the following week. They began their presentation by showing how adult entertainment establishments affect communities. They explained that studies have shown that when adult entertainment businesses congregate in an area, legitimate stores lose business and real estate values plummet. Not only do the adult businesses foster public indecency and prostitution, but crime rates rise dramatically.

They went on to show how to employ zoning and use laws to force these businesses out of the area. For instance, they suggested that the City Council enact legislation pro-hibiting adult use within 500 feet of a school, house of worship, residential area or another adult use establishment. They also suggested that they use current health codes to prove how the sexual activity going on inside these establishments created unsanitary conditions in a public place.

These two modern-day crusaders concluded their presentation by giving each Council member a copy of actual legal verbiage that had been successfully utilized in various cities across the country to rid themselves of sex shops. Their visit was an overwhelming success.

The City Planning Commission subsequently approved amendments to the Zoning Resolution which lined up with those being used elsewhere. Within a few short years of that meeting, the number of adult establishments in the Times Square area had dropped from 57 to just 5, while the number city-wide had decreased from 177 to 29.

As the sleaze was pushed out of Times Square, legitimate businesses took its place. "West 42nd Street was morphing into a ribbon of popular-entertainment venues capitalized by the biggest corporate names in businesses: Disney, Warner Brothers, Sony, AMC, Madame Tussaud's, SFX Entertainment. MTV Networks, and ABC's 'Good Morning America' were broadcasting live a few blocks away.... Real estate values had skyrocketed."[21]

****

The following year, another important issue came to the attention of Bobby Lloyd. He found out that, while it was illegal to produce or distribute child pornography in the state of New York, it was not illegal to possess it.

---

21 As quoted by Lynne B. Sagalyn, *Times Square Roulette,* MIT Press, Cambridge, MA, 2001, p. 7.

A law to close this loophole had been proposed by a state assemblyman, but it had been stalled by the Speaker of the House. Speaker Sheldon Silver had been involved in New York politics for many years. He was first elected to the Assembly in 1976, representing the 64th Assembly District, comprising much of lower Manhattan. By the '90s, he wielded a considerable amount of political clout.

Bobby was undaunted. He was upset about this legal loophole that pedophiles could take advantage of. One day he called one of the Speaker's assistants. "Mr. Smith, there is a bill that has been stalled in committee for months now," Bobby told him in a huff. "It would make the possession of child pornography a felony. Assemblyman Silver is the only one who can get this bill passed at this point, but he continues to stymie every attempt we make to get it passed. Let me tell you something: if he doesn't do something about this, I'm going to hold a press conference in front of your headquarters and I'm going to tell the media that he is for child pornography."

"Mr. Lloyd, I can assure you that Assemblyman Silver is not for child pornography," the legal assistant assured him. "Listen, let me be frank about it. By the time this bill got to committee, other assemblymen had loaded it down with pork barrel projects. We want to get this bill through the Assembly, but we have to get it cleaned up first. Please, give us some time to work on it."

Bobby calmed down as he heard the explanation. "Okay. I hear what you're saying. We'll continue to monitor the situation."

True to his aide's word, Speaker Silver moved the great New York machine and the bill was passed two months later. Although Bobby's political inexperience became evident in the process, he still played a key role in the passage of an important piece of legislation in his home state.

Shortly after, Bobby became friendly with a Long Island Conservative party member, John Andrew Kay. It was through this relationship that Bobby was introduced to and able to navigate through the political arena. Bobby became politically favorable and sought out by many legislators and public figures and eventually became a public policy expert and community advocate and educator.

Mr. Lloyd's expert commentary has been published in *The New York Times* and *Newsday*, and aired on WNBC, WABC, WLIX, Family Radio 103, WMCA, and other TV and Internet talk shows.

Here's what George Cote says about Bobby:

There are very few people in one's life, that it can be said are rich in fellowship and always responsible. I can say without a doubt, Bobby Lloyd is such a friend and co-worker in Christ.

Over twenty years ago, Mary and I were a part of a group working to solve the growing problem of pornography on Long Island, NY. While we were in a meeting of leaders on Long Island, God prompted me that Bobby Lloyd should be the new Executive Director of our efforts. After a full year of searching, meeting, and interviewing, the search committee agreed that Bobby was the best candidate. It was no surprise to me since God had already shown me that he was His choice. For the last 20 plus years, Bobby and Dianne have led, taught, counseled, and saved many lives from the destruction of families due to pornography. (See a photo of the Cote's on page 214.)

Isaiah 58:12 (NKJV) *Those from among you Shall build the old waste places; You shall raise up the foundations of many generations; And you shall be called the Repairer of the Breach, The Restorer of Streets to Dwell In.*

Mayor Giulliani

Sen. Dean Skelos

Congressman King

Town of Babylon
Quality of Life Task Force

Meagan's Law
Senate Hearing

Town Of Babylon Quality Of Life Task Force
PROTECTING OUR COMMUNITIES
Steven Bellone, TOWN SUPERVISOR

Hunt News Conference

Steve Bellone, Town Supervisor

SPOTA

Sen. Johnson

Attn. General Gonzalez

At Ground Zero

Judge Jeanine

Judge John A. Kay & Senator A. Da Motto

IN GOD WE TRUST

Judge John A. Kay & Family

SMOKE SHOP
Cigars • Lotto • Cigarette • Phone Cards

15 closed prostitution rings   2010

Nassau DA   2014

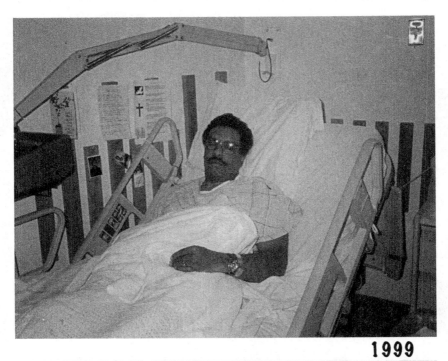

1999

234

CHAPTER TWENTY-NINE

The "C" Word Is Not In My Day-Timer

By the fall of 1998, prospects seemed bright for LICCV. Bobby had engineered, or at least been part of, several celebrated victories. He had pushed through zoning laws in numerous communities on Long Island, causing the closure of a number of adult bookstores. He had also promoted a piece of legislation that eventually made "video peeping"[22] (voyeurism), a crime in New York.

Bobby had also spoken to hundreds of local high school students about the devastating consequences of pornography addiction. He was becoming known and respected throughout political circles of New York. What's more, he was actually receiving a regular salary and was even able to hire a fulltime secretary.

LICCV's annual banquet was to be the climactic event of the year, with Tonya Flynt-Vega as the keynote speaker. As Larry Flynt's daughter, she had experienced firsthand the inside workings of the *Hustler* empire. Years of emotional and sexual abuse at the hands of her father had left her hollow and miserable, but she had found peace through a relationship with Christ. Tonya was now devoting her life to fighting the pornographic industry to which her father belonged.

Bobby was as busy as ever in the weeks leading up to the banquet. And it was during this period that he developed an

---

22   Video taping unsuspecting victims disrobed.

inexplicable obsession with provolone cheese. He ate it every chance he got: on sandwiches, with crackers, or even by itself! What he didn't realize was that it was extremely fattening and in the midst of this two-month binge, he put on 30 pounds.

Meanwhile, he had changed doctors and his new physician, Dr. Dennis Russo, insisted Bobby come in for a complete physical. He reluctantly agreed. A few days after the visit, the Dr. Russo called. "Bobby, you need to get in here right away," he said. "You're missing seven pints of blood."

"Seven pints of blood? What's that mean?"

"I'm not sure, but we need to take more tests."

So that Thursday, the day before their big banquet, Bobby went in for a complete set of X-rays of his internal organs. After examining the film, the doctor told him, "Bobby, these X-rays don't look good. There is some kind of shadow around the area of your pancreas. You need to come in for some more blood work right away."

When Dianne asked Bobby about the X-rays later that day, he downplayed the whole thing. "The doc said I need to come in for some blood work because there's something wrong with the X-ray."

"What?" His explanation didn't make sense to her so she called the doctor herself. "Why does Bobby need blood work?" she asked the doctor.

"What did he tell you?"

"He said he needed it because there's something wrong with the X-ray."

"Dianne, your husband is very sick. He has pancreatic cancer. He needs surgery, but you need to know that he probably won't live more than six months." Dianne collapsed on the couch devastated.

The week after the banquet Bobby and Dianne visited the surgeon whom they had been referred to. He explained the required procedure. They would administer chemotherapy treatments, then they would perform surgery, and afterward, administer another round of chemotherapy to him. The doctor pressed them to submit to the process right away. "This cancer could travel through his system within days. He needs to come in right away."

Something about the man's pushy attitude bothered Dianne, though. For one thing, she wasn't convinced he really knew what he was talking about. She kept asking him how many of these surgeries he had performed, but he kept sidestepping her questions. During the conversation, a thought emerged in her mind: *I bet this surgery will cost $100,000. No wonder he's pressuring us.*

By this point, Bobby just wanted to get the whole thing over with, so he was shocked when Dianne told the doctor they would think about it. Over the next two days, the doctor called them seven different times, pressing them to come in right away. But Dianne knew he was not the surgeon they should go with.

Over the next two months, Bobby endured a number of procedures and spoke with two different surgeons about operating on him. But each time Dianne said she didn't feel right about it. Dr. Damadian, who invented the first MRI machine and a long time supporter of LICCV, heard the news and called Dianne offering an MRI at his facility. He confirmed the diagnosis and firmly suggested Memorial Sloan Kettering, encouraging Dianne to just send them the results of all the tests and get a second opinion. Bobby was uncomfortable with being so far away from home. Dr. Damadian persisted and called again saying, "If it was my wife that's where I would take her."

That settled it for Bobby and Dianne. Unfortunately, they found out that Sloan-Kettering would not accept Bobby's insurance carrier. By now, however, Dianne was convinced that it was the Lord's will for them to use this hospital.

They scheduled an appointment with Dr. Brennan anyway. After reviewing the MRI results, he said brusquely, "You don't need chemo or radiation. If I go in there, I'm going to get it out and it will be clean."

Dianne was hopeful but couldn't understand why his prognosis was so different from what she had been hearing elsewhere. "Why did these other surgeons tell me that Bobby needed chemo and that he could only hope to live another two years?"

"I know what I'm doing," he answered curtly. His words were spoken with such authority that Dianne believed him. On a subsequent visit, she found out that he was the chief of surgery for pancreatic cancer. Her friends weren't exaggerating. He truly was the country's leading surgeon for this type of cancer. After several weeks of appeals, proposals, and pictures pleading for the opportunity to be treated at Sloan, they finally reached the ears of the Executive Offices of HIP, which resulted in Sloan and Hip reaching an agreement to accept payment.

Surgery was scheduled for the following month, February, 1999. Pastor Joe Cedzich drove Bobby and Dianne to the hospital and remained there praying for the entire ten hours of the operation. The surgery was so intense that they had to temporarily remove every vital organ from his body with the exception of his heart and lungs. To do so, they had to cut the tiny connections that held them together.

For six weeks following the surgery, Bobby remained in Sloan-Kettering Hospital with a temperature that hovered over 103 degrees. Apparently there was leakage in those tiny connections they had severed and stitched back together. There was an infection in his body that the doctors were unable to remedy.

For the next several weeks, Bobby was in and out of the hospital. Churches across Long Island kept him at the top of their prayer lists.

One night, Jimmy Jack came to the house to visit. "Bobby, I just feel like I'm supposed to pray for you." For ten minutes his brother-in-law prayed his heart out. It was a mighty prayer of faith. Finally he brought it to a conclusion. "Lord, I pray that you would get rid of this infection from every orifice of his body! I'm believing You to do it! Amen!"

A couple of hours after her brother left, Dianne came into their room to dress him for bed. Bobby was not able to care for himself yet. She happened to brush her hand across his stomach and he jumped. "What's wrong?" she asked, pulling up his shirt. There on his abdomen a huge purple lump had appeared. "Wow! What's that?"

"I dunno," Bobby answered, exhausted by the ordeal.

"I'll take you back to Sloan-Kettering in the morning."

The next morning she came back into the room to find Bobby in a pool of blood. There was a three-inch hole in his stomach where the lump had been. Dianne quietly taped sanitary napkins all over his abdomen to soak up the flow of blood. She quickly got the boys off to school, not wanting to alarm them. They were so ecstatic their dad was finally home. She immediately called Sloan and was instructed to bring him in STAT! If he began to hemorrhage, bring him to the nearest hospital. She drove him straight to Sloan.

When they arrived, Dr. Brennan and several nurses were awaiting them. As soon as they saw his stomach—and much to the shock of the panicked couple—they all broke into applause.

The grinning doctor explained the outburst of exuberance. "Don't you see, Dianne? The infection has finally found its way out of Bobby's body. He's going to be okay now!"

And sure enough, during the following weeks Bobby began to grow stronger. One day, nearly three months after the surgery, he was actually able to eat a little food.

"Bobby, now I understand the obsession with provolone!" Dianne suddenly announced.

"What are you talking about?" Bobby asked weakly.

"You gained 30 pounds eating that stuff," she said. "You have lost 50 pounds since the operation. If you wouldn't have had that extra weight, you might not have made it!"

Bobby had survived the most traumatic event of his life, but he would discover soon enough that it came at great expense to his body.

The Lloyds with Jimmy & Miriam
2015

Bobby & Attn. General Ashcroft

Gallagher & Lloyd

CHAPTER THIRTY

Deeper and Wider

The trauma Bobby's body endured through the entire episode greatly weakened him physically and emotionally. But there was a silver lining in the cancer cloud that Bobby didn't see for a long time. While his work for LICCV suffered because of the physical limitations he faced, the experience immensely furthered his spiritual growth. What he went through did more to humble him than a thousand sermons on the detrimental effects of pride in a person's life could have accomplished.

It took months for him to regain enough strength to return to the office. But before long, Bobby was back fighting for the decency of his community.

In March, 2001, two years after his operation, he was part of a delegation of a dozen pro-family activists that were invited to meet with Attorney General John Ashcroft in the Justice Department.

The men gathered around a huge conference table and began to share their concerns about the effects pornography was having on the culture. During the whole time they were speaking, Attorney General Ashcroft had his head down and was writing on a tablet. At first Bobby thought he was just ignoring them, working on something else, but eventually it became apparent he was taking careful notes of everything said.

Nevertheless, about an hour into it, the meeting seemed to hit a lull. It was as if nothing they said had any effect on the Attorney General. Then Jerry Kirk turned to Bobby and asked him to share his testimony. Bobby spent a few minutes talking about his addiction to pornography and how it had warped his perspectives on sexuality. The meeting continued on for a few more minutes before concluding. It seemed like a complete failure.

As the men stood around in small groups talking, Bobby approached the Attorney General. "Mr. Ashcroft, can I have a minute to share my heart with you?"

"Yes, of course."

"Mr. Ashcroft, if the government does not get involved in this issue, we've got a problem," Bobby said emphatically. "If pornography continues on unchecked the way it has, it is going to destroy every bit of decency left in this country. My life is an example of how it can destroy a life. If Jesus Christ hadn't intervened in my life, who knows where I would be today."

"And there's another issue that I'm very concerned about," Bobby continued. "Child pornography has really increased on the internet. We have to do something about it because it is fostering a mindset that is victimizing our children."

"Yes, I know you're right, Bobby. We'll see what we can do," he answered.

Little did Bobby know, but two months prior to this meeting Attorney General Ashcroft had authorized a major investigation of a group of pedophiles who were sharing obscene pictures of children via the internet. Within months, Operation Candyman busted up an "e-group" of 7,000 members, most of whom were Americans. Forty people were arrested in 26 states.

****

The month after the meeting at the Justice Department, another significant event occurred in the life of Bobby Lloyd. Through his brother-in-law, Jimmy Jack, Bobby had been introduced to a ministry in Kentucky that had pioneered the country's first residential program for sex addicts. Similar to Jimmy's work with drug addicts at Long Island Teen Challenge, Steve Gallagher and the dedicated staff of Pure Life Ministries had been ministering to sex addicts for many years.

For the past several years, the staff of Pure Life Ministries (PLM) had been setting aside a week for fasting, culminating with one full day for seeking the Lord. In April, 2001, the leadership of PLM decided to change things a bit, opening up this time to others outside the ministry, and inviting David Ravenhill and Doug Detert[23] to be keynote speakers for three days of special meetings. As they had in years past, the staff fasted for several days leading up to the weekend and then designated the first day of the conference to be spent seeking the Lord.

Urged by his brother-in-law, Bobby decided to attend, but the weekend wasn't what he had expected. He was accustomed to fast-paced meetings, with loud music and a lot of emotion. By contrast, the PLM conference was quiet and worshipful. The small gathering literally spent hours waiting on the Lord, the silence broken only by brief periods of crying out to Him for His presence. But the most challenging part of it for Bobby was the style of preaching. David Ravenhill and Doug Detert are both thoughtful men with a deep message. Neither is given to emotional appeals or sensational preaching.

During the final day of the conference, Bobby sat in the back row of the church, unimpressed and somewhat detached. *Just a little longer and I'm outta here*, he thought to himself. Doug Detert had just spoken, but now the leaders felt led to sit in silence, just

---

23 David Ravenhill is an itinerant pastor, very much in the mold of his father, Leonard Ravenhill. Doug Detert is a lesser known Pentecostal pastor from Zion Faith Homes in Illinois who played a key role in the spiritual development of the leadership at Pure Life Ministries.

quietly waiting on the Lord. *Man, these guys are boring,* he began fuming inside. *Why am I here? And why do we have to sit here in silence for a whole hour? This is ridiculous!*

As Bobby stewed in his critical spirit, a strong word from the Lord came forth from one of the ministers. "The Lord wants to do a deep work inside someone here right now!"

All of the sudden, it was as if Bobby became encapsulated in some kind of spiritual bubble. He was still sitting there, but he couldn't hear what was going on around him. Then the voice of the Lord penetrated his mind. "Let it go. Just let it go," He told Bobby.

"What do you mean, Lord?" Bobby asked.

The Lord didn't answer his question directly, but he felt something powerful take hold of him inside. Then his mind became filled with the reality of Jesus Christ. The lack of his resemblance to Christ was inescapable and devastating. *I'm nothing but filthy rags. I'm not in a good place spiritually. I'm full of pride and selfishness. I continually keep the Lord at a distance. I won't make myself vulnerable to Him or anyone else.* On and on the convicting thoughts flowed into his mind. There simply was no refuting the truth about his lack of humility, love, and consecration.

As he became overwhelmed about his spiritual condition, an intense groan started welling up from the deepest parts of his being. Before he even knew it, he was sobbing profusely. He realized that it was his pride the Lord was asking him to release.

Then, as if an unseen hand stood him upright, he got to his feet right in the middle of the meeting. There stood this proud ex-gangster, convulsing in tears, sobbing uncontrollably in front of several hundred people—bringing the meeting to a halt. Steve Gallagher, PLM's founder, went back and laid hands on Bobby and began praying that God would do a deep work inside him. The prayer set off another round of tears as his groans grew louder.

God put Bobby Lloyd in his place during that meeting. From that day on, there was a noticeable change in his behavior toward others. In the past, he had gotten by on his personal charisma and natural abilities with people. But many of those he interacted with had no idea how he secretly disdained them. He was outwardly friendly, but his heart was cold toward them. There were other times he would slight a person in front of others or simply ignore him. Most of all, he never, ever allowed himself to be vulnerable in front of other people.

But after that experience, Bobby was much more compassionate toward others. His voice, countenance, and mannerisms all softened. People became more comfortable around him. This was especially true of those who knew him best. His relationship blossomed with his daughters, Dawn, Monique, Chante and Bobbette. There were even times that he allowed them to vent their anger toward him for the lack of love he had shown them during their lives. He began to enjoy his children and grandchildren in new ways, not mechanically or awkwardly as in the past.

The most meaningful change in his life though, was in his relationship with God. The truth is that he had had very little trust for the Lord. He followed Him, but it was always at a safe distance, where he could remain in control. This all changed. He saw that the nagging doubts about God that had kept him on the fence of indecision over the years came out of a lack of trust in Him. He had determined at a young age that he would never trust anyone but himself, and that attitude followed him into Christianity.

His faith grew much stronger. Before that day, he would fret over finances and scheme to make things happen. But a quiet confidence in the Lord was now lodged in his heart. When he faced problems or setbacks, he *knew* he only needed to turn to his Father in prayer and everything would work out. Yes, Bobby Lloyd was a different man not just outwardly, but inwardly as well.

****

In the fall of 2007, Bobby and Dianne had decided to honor a supportive local politician during LICCV's annual banquet. Bobby got up in front of the hundreds of people in attendance and asked Assemblyman Andrew Raia to join him at the podium.

He began to express his gratitude to the Assemblyman when the man suddenly interrupted him. "Excuse me, Bobby," Assemblyman Raia said. "But actually I would rather talk about you."

Bobby was surprised and unsure of how to respond to this unexpected interruption in the agenda. The politician continued undaunted. "Bobby, I have with me the Excelsior Award which I have been authorized by the New York State Assembly to present to you tonight. It is the highest award the State of New York has to confer upon an individual for work on behalf of our state."

"Allow me to read part of it," he continued. "Whereas Robert Lloyd has committed himself to the elimination of sexual violence and the victimization of children, women, and families in the Long Island Metropolitan area... and has been instrumental in assisting and supporting government agencies in drafting legislation and initiating laws that protect those who are most vulnerable against sexual violence, as well as the exploitation of women and children.... Resolved, That as a duly elected Member of the State Assembly of New York and on behalf of the residents of the Ninth Assembly District, on the Fifth Day of October in the year Two

Thousand Seven, I congratulate and commend Robert Lloyd as an individual that is worthy of the esteem of both his community and the people of New York State."

The award was from a secular government, of course, but it was also a fitting tribute to the tremendous transformation of character that had occurred in Bobby's life. There was a time when he had been a notorious gangster and parasite on the communities of Long Island. He had hurt many people in the midst of his selfish pursuits. But God laid hold of Bobby's heart, broke him of his selfishness, and humbled him in the dust. Only the Holy Spirit could have transformed him from street-hustling gangster to crusading activist and devout man of God.

Assemblyman Andrew Raia presenting the Excelcious Award

Greg & Mom at Monique's wedding
1996

Greg & Mom at his own Wedding
1992

Gregg's Angels
2015

Gregg & wife, Audrey, and their girls
2013

Gregg & Mom at Shekinah Hair Salon
1989

Gregg studying
1995

CHAPTER THIRTY-ONE

His Ways Are Not Our Ways

At 11:48 on a Saturday night, the 21st of September, 2013 the phone rang. Dianne could hear the caller ID Audrey Wrobel, Greg's wife. Dianne, in her mother's heart, knew. She raced to the kitchen to pick up the landline. Audrey, distraught and talking rapidly, explained she just received a phone call from one of Greg's friends from Oceanside. He was at a barbecue of his school colleagues and passed out and can't drive, would Dianne go and get him? Of course, she would. She quickly called Bobby who was downstairs. Get dressed! We have to go get Greg in Oceanside repeating what Audrey said.

As she dressed, going over the conversation in her head with Audrey, she called the number Audrey gave her. A woman answered. Dianne explained that she would be there in about half hour to pick up Greg. The woman seemed confused, "You are going to pick him up?

"Yes," Dianne said. "I am his mother. I understand he cannot drive. My husband and I will be right there. What is your address in Oceanside?"

The woman said, "We are not in Oceanside. We are in Babylon and the ambulance is here. We got him out of the pool and got him breathing. They are ready to take him now."

Dianne's heart stopped. "Must be his asthma. What happened?"

The woman explained. "Greg was horsing around, jumping in and out of the pool. Then he dove in and wasn't moving. We thought he was kidding. We dragged him out. He wasn't breathing.

We did CPR and got him breathing. Meet him at the Emergency room."

Frantically, Dianne got dressed, packing some essentials since it was going to be a long night. Dianne called and explained the details to Audrey who was still foggy from sleep. Immediately Audrey was alert and said, "Come get me!"

Bobby left to pick up Audrey while Dianne drove directly to the ER. After getting off the exit, much to her surprise, she was behind an ambulance! Could it be? Yes it was! West Babylon Fire Department Rescue.

Riding along side of the vehicle, her mother's heart aching, she called on the God of Heaven who had delivered and saved her so many years before. She followed the ambulance right into the ER parking lot. Barely stopping her car, she jutted out to the gurney holding her only born child's lifeless body. She reached out to touch his foot hanging off the gurney, touching it gently. The hands of a police officer stopped her, escorting her into the waiting area where a doctor grabbed both of her hands. Gently speaking to her, he ensured her they would get him settled and come for her.

Moments later Audrey arrived. They embraced and began to pray. Shortly after a doctor, nurse, social worker, and a priest came in the waiting area. Mother and daughter braced themselves for the news. Greg had broken his neck. He was not responding. They would know better in 24 hours. The priest offered to go pray for Greg. Dianne explained that her husband and brother were on their way. "They are pastors and I am an ordained minister myself." Immediately the priest took her by the hand to the trauma room. He escorted her to Greg's side. She looked at her beautiful, handsome boy. The nurses and doctors scurried around her. Dianne anointed his head with oil and whispered in his ear. "It's

Mommy. I'm here. Call on the name of Jesus, Jesus, Jesus." After praying, she quietly turned and left her son in the hands of God her Heavenly Father, and the doctors.

For five long days there was a parade of loved ones, students, and clergy that came to join forces with the Lloyds for the life of their beloved eldest son. Dianne kept a 24 hour prayer vigil at his bedside as Audrey comforted their three beautiful teen age daughters and was forced to make high risk medical decisions for her childhood sweet heart whose life hung in the balance.

On September 25, 2013 Audrey, Bobby, Dianne, and Greg's daughters heard the words that their beloved Greg had gone home to heaven. Life would never be the same.

They had the privilege to usher him to glory on his birthday at the most wonderful Celebration of Life on October 3, 2013 at Bethlehem Assembly of God, Valley Stream, NY.

Thus began another season in the life of Bobby and Dianne; how would they survive such a traumatic event?

Bobby and Dianne have pressed into the Lord, embracing the Word of God that has been their life-line through their turbulent life—being so grateful for all He has done in their life and family. So thankful for all Greg accomplished in his 45 years of life and his commitment to Christ, knowing that it was God who blessed them with Greg and kept Greg from the life style that they were delivered from.

The entire family leans on the scripture Isaiah 55:8-9

> "For my thoughts are not your thoughts, neither are your ways my ways,"declares the LORD. "As the heavens are higher than the earth so are my ways higher than your ways and my thoughts than your thoughts.

This experience has brought them both to a deeper relationship with Christ, enriching them and empowering them to continue in the work that He has equipped them to do.

Bobby and Dianne and all their children exemplify the life-changing miracles of God. These eight children having four different mothers and four different fathers have all come to the knowledge of Christ. The majority of them serve the Lord in some capacity in their home churches, Most have degrees ranging from BA's to Masters. Three, at this writing, are preparing to work toward their Doctorates! The Lord blessed them with sixteen grandchildren including, 5 great grandchildren. Their quiver is full! Bobby and his family continue to shine forth as living testimonies to the fact that the Lord can take the most hopeless life and transform it into one that exhibits His glory.

Together, Bobby and Dianne continue to serve the Lord in ministry by working to protect women, children, families, and the community from the harmful effects of pornography and the sexualized culture on Long Island and the New York metropolitan area. They have become experts in their field and are seasoned speakers who cross all racial, religious, and cultural lines. Bobby and Dianne are in demand locally, statewide, and nationwide, sharing the life-changing message Christ has put on their hearts to a lost and dying world.

Gregg leading worship
2010

I'm Coming Home!

ISAIAH 55:8-9

Gregory Walter Wrobel Jr., born on October 3, 1968 at Mercy Hospital in Rockville Centre, NY weighing in at 7lbs 4oz. has passed into Glory!

Greg Wrobel or "Wrobel as he was affectionately called by his hundreds of students died Wednesday September 25, 2013 at North Shore LIJ of injuries sustained in a swimming accident at a outdoor barbecue.

Wrobel a teacher certified in three Sciences taught in the Castleton Alternative High School in Oceanside for over 12 years. He was hailed throughout the years for his creative and cooperative teaching skills. Sometimes his ways were unorthodox, to say the least, however, he had a gift to connect with his troubled students through his humorous, innovative style which enabled him to relate to them on their level. Also to his advantage was his stature, 6 foot, weighing in at 220lbs, long wavey hair, a little goate. A T-shirt and Jeans was his attire. The students knowing he benched pressed 300lbs of dead weight was something they strongly considered before they challenged his authority.

A troubled youth himself with much the same background as his students, he was determined to help them to excel not only in science but in life itself. At times he shared his challenging background with them to prove we all have choices in life. We may not choose how we came into the world but we have a choice what we do with what we were given.

Born to teen age parents, Greg lived with his grandparents for the majority of his life in Rockville Centre. Both his parents, Greg and Dianne, shared in his rearing and imparted their many giftings to him throughout the years. His father's humor and fishing and hunting skills would later lead him to a teaching career in science. His aunt and uncle, Jeanette and Gaspar Geluso, would add much needed stability and structure to his life.

He attended St. Agnes Elementary School and graduated from the eighth grade. It was at this time he received his first guitar, which would lead him to become a passionate song writer, musician, music producer, and worship leader.

He continued his secondary education at South Side High School, graduating by the skin of his teeth. It was during this time that his mother made a life changing decision to become a Christian and live her life for God.

Greg also made that decision at a very young age. He attended church and youth group faithfully, studied the Bible, and dragged all his friends and any one who would listen to church to hear about this God who could change your life.

Upon graduating high school, he chose to follow in the footsteps of his mother Dianne who had become a very successful hairdresser in Oceanside. He attended Long Island Beauty School in Baldwin and acquired his NYS hairdresser's license. Greg apprenticed in many high end salons on the norh shore eventually ending up working as a hair dresser with his mom. Together they opened Shekinah Hair Salon, a Christian owned and operated business in Oceanside.

It was at Shekinah Hair Salon that he would meet his future wife Audrey, the girl of his dreams. Audrey attended Christ for the Nations Bible Institute in Stoney Brook with his maternal grandmother Adele Jack. Grandma brought Audrey to Shekinah to met her handsome grandson and it was love at first sight. Audrey decided to go to beauty school and become a hairdresser also. Audrey attended beauty school and began apprenticing on 5ht Ave in Manhattan.

Greg and Audrey began attending Bethlehem Assembly of God together in Valley Stream and quickly became youth leaders under the leadership of Pastor Steve Millazo. Greg became a passionate disciple, mentoring the many younger believers until they could walk alone

In July of 1992, Greg and Audrey were married and were both working at Shekinah Hair Salon. However they began to get weary and desired something different in their life. Much to all of their parents surprise, they decided to go out of state to college and attend Evangel University in Missouri, to become teachers.

It was there that they would add two beautiful ladies to their family, Elizabeth and Rebekah. Greg excelled in college holding a 3.5 or better throughout and graduating Magna Cum Laude! With much help from Audrey's parents, in four years they both graduated with two degrees. With their two children, they were on their way home to start a new life.

Audrey's father was a city school teacher, and with his help again Greg nailed down a teaching job in Queens. He quickly began working on his accreditation and Masters Degree. Completing his Master in Science from Adelfi University in 2001.

They purchased their first home in Lynbrook and then along came their final bundle of joy, Rachel. The Quiver was full, and it was time for Greg to move on to bigger and better things.

With his Masters in Education and certification in three sciences he was ready for the big time. Out went the resumes. Many nerve raking interviews followed, and finally an interview at Oceanside High School. Male science teachers were hard to find, especially those that were certified in three sciences, so Greg could have had the cream of the crop job, but he chose Castleton High School because he wanted to make a difference in young people's lives who were much like him. He also had another reason: his maternal grandfather was in the Hall of Fame of Oceanside High School.

The rest is history. He touched the lives of thousands of students over the years, not only making an impact in their lives educationally but personally also.

While in the hospital for nearly a week after the incident, fighting valiantly for his life, there was a parade of student, family, and friends telling story after story about the pivotal experiences they had with Greg Wrobel that changed their lives forever.

On that fateful day when his family heard the news that their Champion was no longer with them, they were invited to join a vigil at the Castleton High School in Oceanside where hundreds of students gathered for a prayer vigil, lead by the students themselves and Fran Gilespi and Ed Dempsey, co-teachers with Wrobel. Candles, pictures, and balloons adorned the steps of the school where Wrobel was hailed as a hero. Students, teachers, family, and friends gathered to tell stories of the teacher that changed the course of their lives. After hours of memories, tears, and laughter, a beautiful prayer and farewell were offered by Ed Dempsey and scores of white balloons were released to the music of Nervana.

Greg leaves behind his wife Audrey, their three daughters, Elizabeth, 18, Rebekah, 16, and Rachel 13; his father, Greg Wrobel and his wife Nan, and his paternal siblings, Stephanie, Jessica and Matt; his mother, Dianne Lloyd and husband, Bobby and his maternal siblings, Paula, Monique, Chante, Dawn, Bobbette, Daniel and Robert and countless aunts, uncles, cousins, nieces, and nephews

GREG WROBEL

10/03/68 — 9/25/13

AUDREY

ELIZABETH, BEKKY, RACHEL

258

EPILOGUE
IN
PICTURES

The Lloyd family

2012

2008

2015

Bobby and his Daughters

2000

1998

1989

Rob and Dan

Daughters and Family

Chante's Family
2014

Bobbette's Family
2015

Dawn & Deputy Chief, Mark
2013

Dawn & Monique
2013

Monique getting Teacher's Award
2012

Monique
2014

Rob and Daniel All Grown Up

Daniel & Fiance, Charlotte
2014

Rob with Greg's wife, Audrey
2015

Rob and Daughter, Destiny

2014

2015

Bobby's Siblings

With Pop and Stevie   1992

Bobby's Paternal Half-Sisters

Pat   Timolin

Meet The Grandchildren

Gregg's girls and newest granddaughter, Rory

Shamilia and her five children with Paula

Rob's Destiny

Destiny and her mom, Jessica

Mark, Dawn, and their family

Thank you for reading *Black Knight*. If Bobby Lloyd's story has blessed you in any way, we would appreciate your taking a moment to write a review on Amazon, as well as on other sites like Barnes and Noble, Christian Book, Olive Press Publisher, and on social media. If we get 50 reviews on Amazon, then Amazon will include *Black Knight* in their promotions, such as, "Customers who bought this item also bought...."

Thank you for helping this book get the exposure it needs!

Black Knight

is available at:

olivepresspublisher.com

amazon.com

barnesandnoble.com

christianbook.com

deepershopping.com

and other online stores

Store managers:

Order wholesale through:

Ingram Book Company or

Spring Arbor

or by emailing:

olivepressbooks@gmail.com

To Contact the author:

Long Island Citizens for Community Values (LICCV)
Office phone: 631-608-3778
www.liccv.org

CPSIA information can be obtained
at www.ICGtesting.com
Printed in the USA
LVOW04s2133271116
514688LV00016B/240/P

9 781941 173138